Angelic Encounters by James and Michal Ann Goll is a must-read for those who are hungry to grow in their understanding of the invisible kingdom of God. This book is extremely inspirational and easy to read, and yet it can also be used as a textbook on the subject. Read *Angelic Encounters*, and then...have some.

—PATRICIA KING
EXTREME PROPHETIC

With solid biblical teaching and an eye for the prophetic activity in our day, James W. and Michal Ann Goll have brought us a masterpiece in their latest book, *Angelic Encounters*. This book will add discernment, wisdom, and understanding to each one who has an ear to hear.

—DR. CHÉ AHN
HARVEST INTERNATIONAL MINISTRIES
AUTHOR, *Fire Evangelism*

Who hasn't longed to have an encounter with one of God's angels? This book by my friends James and Michal Ann Goll will inform, delight, and make you hungry for more of God's supernatural intervention in your life. They did a superb job in weaving biblical examples with contemporary ones while illustrating what a multifaceted lot God's angels really are. It's a book I want to keep in my library for future research. I think you will, too.

—QUIN SHERRER
COAUTHOR, *Lord, I Need to Pray With Power*

If ever you have wished for answers to puzzling questions about angels, this book is a must-read! Not only do James and Michal Ann provide sound biblical teaching about the nature and function of angels, but they also share countless stories about angelic visitations, both their own and testimonies of others. It's a wonderful resource for Bible studies.

—RUTHANNE GARLOCK
COAUTHOR, *Lord, I Need Your Healing Power*

Everything you ever wanted to know about angels can be found in this newest book by the Golls! Drawing from Scripture, James and Michal Ann lay a biblical foundation for this important topic and present us with a book that can actually be used as a reference work on angels. They also share experiences from their own lives as well as the lives of many others who have had encounters with the angelic realm. Not just a fascinating read, this book will leave you hungering for the supernatural realm in your life.

—Jane Hansen
President/CEO, Aglow International

Angelic Encounters is another timely book from James and Michal Ann Goll. Supernatural experiences are increasing all around us. We are in great need of instruction to help us clarify and understand the visitations that are becoming more and more common. While it is foolish to worship angels, it is equally foolish to ignore them. The Golls have given us the much-needed instruction that will prove helpful in enabling us to correctly steward this great day of heavenly invasions.

—Bill Johnson
Senior Pastor, Bethel Church
Author, *When Heaven Invades Earth*

My first meeting with James Goll was through a recording where he talked about the opening of the portal resulting in Jacob's encounter with angels in Genesis 28. That recording leapt in my spirit and compelled within me a desire to meet James Goll. Now James and Michal Ann have written this incredible book about what has become commonplace yet divine for them and others. We are living in an age when heaven has never been closer to Earth. This includes the awareness of and encounters with angels. This book will build your faith for all God has for us in this season.

—Barbara J. Yoder
Senior Pastor, Shekinah Christian Church
Ann Arbor, MI

A N G E L I C
Encounters

James W. & Michal Ann Goll

Charisma
HOUSE
A STRANG COMPANY

Most STRANG COMMUNICATIONS/CHARISMA HOUSE/SILOAM/FRONTLINE/ REALMS products are available at special quantity discounts for bulk purchase for sales promotions, premiums, fund-raising, and educational needs. For details, write Strang Communications/Charisma House/Siloam/FrontLine/ Realms, 600 Rinehart Road, Lake Mary, Florida 32746, or telephone (407) 333-0600.

ANGELIC ENCOUNTERS by James W. and Michal Ann Goll
Published by Charisma House
A Strang Company
600 Rinehart Road
Lake Mary, Florida 32746
www.charismahouse.com

Cover Design: The DesignWorks Group, Charles Brock,
www.thedesignworksgroup.com
Cover Image: iStockphoto.com, Linus Sebastian
Executive Design Director: Bill Johnson

Library of Congress Cataloging-in-Publication Data:

Goll, Jim W.
  Angelic encounters / by James W. and Michal Ann Goll. -- 1st ed.
     p. cm.
  Includes bibliographical references and index.
  ISBN 978-1-59979-065-7 (trade paper)
  1. Angels--Christianity. 2. Visions. I. Goll, Michal Ann. II. Title.
  BT966.3.G65 2007
  235'.3--dc22

                                                    2007002164

First Edition

07 08 09 10 11 — 987654321
Printed in the United States of America

We would like to dedicate this book to our mothers who marked our lives with prayer and consecration to the Lord Jesus Christ. They both now make up a part of the great cloud of witnesses who have gone on before us. We love and miss you!

- **Amanda Elizabeth (Burns) Goll**, mother of James W. Goll

- **Dorris Grace (McCoy) Willard**, mother of Michal Ann Goll

You shaped our lives to be who we are today!

Acknowledgments

Every book that we compose is like having another child. A lot of love and nurture go into each birthing. Midwives also help deliver the goods, and in this project we have a few that we would like to acknowledge.

First, we want to thank the Lord for Bert Ghezzi, the former editorial director of Charisma House, and all the current staff of this great publishing company. Kathy Deering, our dear writing partner with this project, is one of heaven's great gems in the earth. We also want to thank the Lord for the sacrificial service from the staff of Encounters Network and Compassion Acts who hold up our hands in a constant and consistent manner. Your labors of love are noticed, and we give thanks to the Lord for each and every one of you!

Contents

Foreword

The first time I met James Goll, he looked at me with his piercing eyes and asked a probing question: "Lee, do you have enough people praying for you?"

We were driving through the streets of downtown Atlanta together, headed to a banquet for authors and publishers. But when Jim posed this odd question, I quickly lost track of time and place. It seemed as if he were looking past the moving scenery and into an invisible, eternal realm. I knew he could see something I couldn't.

"Why do you say that?" I asked, knowing that I have always felt awkward asking people to pray for me on a regular basis.

"I really feel you need more prayer covering," Jim said. "It's urgent. With all that you are involved in, you are a target of the enemy. You must recruit more intercessors."

Our conversation shifted to other matters during that evening, but I couldn't stop thinking about Jim's prophetic directive. I trusted his words because I knew God was speaking to him. And I knew Jim could see that something was missing in my life. I needed to ask the Lord for angelic protection.

As soon as I got home from that trip I became bolder about asking for prayer support. Every time I preached somewhere I asked intercessors to commit to praying regularly for my family and my overseas travels. Within a year I had more than one hundred prayer warriors backing me up.

These prayer warriors were praying for me when I was in Muslim-dominated areas of northern Nigeria, when I was among Indonesia's largest unreached people group, and when I was challenging the spiritual strongholds of domestic violence in Guatemala and El Salvador. I have now preached in more than twenty nations and have always felt a blanket of invisible protection over me—even when a South American dictator once kicked my colleagues and me out of our conference venue so he could hold a political rally.

God has always stationed His angels around me, and I have no doubt that those same angels helped me obtain passports, visas, and lost sermon notes; strengthened me against sickness and disease; stabilized airplanes during turbulence; hid me from thieves, thugs, and scam artists; shielded my house from hurricane winds; and fought off demonic missiles that were headed in my direction.

I have actually never seen the angels that protect me, but that doesn't mean they aren't there. Faith, according to the Bible, is the evidence of things not seen (Heb. 11:1). I know God has stationed His armies around the righteous who are doing His will.

But there are certainly times when God opens the eyes of His people to see what He is doing in the supernatural realm. And Jim and Michal Ann Goll, as prophets to the body of Christ, have been given this ability so that they can encourage us all to experience the miraculous.

Jim Goll is what some people call a seer, a prophet with a special gift from the Holy Spirit that enables him to see into the invisible realm. This ability has nothing to do with the occult. It is a gift Paul mentioned in his letter to the Corinthians:

> For to one is given the word of wisdom through the Spirit, and to another the word of knowledge according to the same Spirit; to another faith by the same Spirit, and to another gifts of healing by the one Spirit, and to another the effecting of miracles, and to another prophecy, *and to another the distinguishing of spirits*, to another various kinds of tongues, and to another the interpretation of tongues.
>
> —1 Corinthians 12:8–10, emphasis added

Those who operate at the highest level of discernment of spirits are able to see into the invisible realm. They can see the angels of God, and they also can perceive the work of demonic spirits. Armed with keen eagle vision, they can see through God's eyes by the Holy Spirit so that they can expose the strategies of the devil's forces and also commission God's angelic warriors for battle.

Many of us trudge through life only living by what our eyes see. We may become discouraged because of circumstances and difficulties. If only we could see into the invisible realm! We would discover that God has been warring in the heavenlies over our situation. We would see that angels have been fighting for us and shielding us from danger.

In the Old Testament, we learn that the prophet Elisha's attendant was worried about the encroaching armies of Aram. He cried out to Elisha, "What shall we do?" (2 Kings 6:15).

Elisha offered assurance to his disciple and said, "Do not fear, for those who are with us are more than those who are with them" (v. 16). Those words may not have been too convincing if Elisha's assistant had only looked at what he saw in the natural. Aram's armies looked fierce and intimidating. The circumstances looked bleak. But the Bible tells us in 2 Kings 6:17:

> Then Elisha prayed and said, "O Lord, I pray, open his eyes, that he may see." And the Lord opened the servant's eyes and he saw; and behold, the mountain was full of horses and chariots of fire all around Elisha.

When I read this passage about Elisha, I think of James and Michal Ann Goll. Like Elisha, they have been blessed to see what many of us cannot discern. They have known the power of God's angels, and they have seen them on many occasions. And just as Elisha longed for his servant to see the flaming armies of heaven, the Golls are eager for us to see into this supernatural realm. That is why they have written this book—to help open your eyes to the reality of angels and to teach you how to experience all the benefits of God's angelic protection.

I pray that as you read this book your eyes will indeed be opened to the unseen realm. May you suddenly recognize that your Father's heavenly army surrounds you and that your enemies have been outnumbered by heaven's victorious forces.

—J. LEE GRADY
EDITOR, *Charisma* MAGAZINE
DIRECTOR, THE MORDECAI PROJECT

Blessed assurance, Jesus is mine!
Oh, what a foretaste of glory divine!
Heir of salvation, purchase of God,
Born of His Spirit, washed in His blood.
Perfect submission, perfect delight,
Visions of rapture now burst on my sight;
Angels descending bring from above
Echoes of mercy, whispers of love.[1]

O N E

Jacob's Ladder Keeps
Coming Down

Who could have imagined? Heaven opened up and visitors came down for an earthly visit. They revealed God's intentions, and they made promises (and the promises came true).

The man who was privileged to receive the angelic visitors did not seem to deserve such a high honor. As a matter of fact, his character was seriously flawed. He had conspired with his mother, cheated his older brother, and even deceived his ailing father. The night the angels came down, he was running like a fugitive from his home, from his God, and from his own true calling, destiny, and identity. The night with the angels changed all that.

Jacob was destined to become the father of the twelve great tribes of Israel, but he was on the run from Beersheba to Haran, which was twelve miles north of Jerusalem. Night fell, so he found a rock for a pillow and, exhausted, sank into a deep sleep. He began to dream. Now, you might think that having gone off to sleep in such a disturbed condition, he might have had nightmares, full of tension and anxiety. God would have been justified in giving him dreams full of stern admonitions about honesty, truthfulness, and obedience, dreams that would have warned him about the certain penalty for his enormous sins.

Instead, a gracious God gave Jacob a glimpse of heaven coming down to Earth. This man named Jacob, who was a deceiver and a supplanter, saw a sight that few others have seen. God's own illumination lit up the darkness, stretching from heaven to Earth and back again. Jacob beheld the transcendent beauty of the Lord God. Ministering angels—too many to count—moved down and up on a heavenly ladder or staircase. Jacob was dreaming, but the angels were real.

How do we know they were real? Because of his profound reaction to this experience. Here's how the scriptural account reads:

> Then Jacob departed from Beersheba and went toward Haran. He came to a certain place and spent the night there, because the sun had set; and he took one of the stones of the place and put it under his head, and lay down in that place.
>
> He had a dream, and behold, a ladder was set on the earth with its top reaching to heaven; and behold, the angels of God were ascending and descending on it. And behold, the LORD stood above it and said, "I am the LORD, the God of your father Abraham and the God of Isaac; the land on which you lie, I will give it to you and to your descendants.
>
> "Your descendants will also be like the dust of the earth, and you will spread out to the west and to the east and to the north and to the south; and in you and in your descendants shall all the families of the earth be blessed.
>
> "Behold, I am with you and will keep you wherever you go, and will bring you back to this land; for I will not leave you until I have done what I have promised you."
>
> Then Jacob awoke from his sleep and said, "Surely the LORD is in this place, and I did not know it." He was afraid and said, "How awesome is this place! This is none other than the house of God, and this is the gate of heaven."
>
> So Jacob rose early in the morning, and took the stone that he had put under his head and set it up as a pillar and poured oil on its top. He called the name of that place Bethel; however, previously the name of the city had been Luz.

Then Jacob made a vow, saying, "If God will be with me and will keep me on this journey that I take, and will give me food to eat and garments to wear, and I return to my father's house in safety, then the LORD will be my God. This stone, which I have set up as a pillar, will be God's house, and of all that You give me I will surely give a tenth to You."

—Genesis 28:10–22

Jacob was blown away. He had had an encounter with God Himself, who stood at the top of the heavenly ladder, directing everything so that the generational blessing and destiny He had promised to Jacob's grandfather would be fulfilled. Here's how it is described in *Matthew Henry's Commentary:*

Angels are employed as ministering spirits, to serve all the purposes and designs of Providence, and the wisdom of God is at the upper end of the ladder, directing all the motions of second causes to the glory of the first Cause. The angels are active spirits, continually ascending and descending; they rest not, day nor night, from service, according to the posts assigned them. They ascend, to give account of what they have done, and to receive orders; and then descend, to execute the orders they have received. Thus we should always abound in the work of the Lord, that we may do it as the angels do it, (Ps. 103:20–21). This vision gave very seasonable comfort to Jacob, letting him know that he had both a good guide and a good guard, in his going out and coming in,—that, though he was made to wander from his father's house, yet still he was the care of a kind Providence, and the charge of the holy angels....Jacob was now the type and representative of the whole church, with the guardianship of which the angels are entrusted....

(1) God's manifestations of himself to his people carry their own evidence along with them. God can give undeniable demonstrations of his presence, such as give abundant satisfaction to the souls of the faithful that God is with them of a truth, satisfaction not communicable to others, but convincing to themselves.

(2) We sometimes meet with God where we little thought of meeting with him. He is where we did not think he had been, is found where we asked not for him. No place excludes divine visits (Gen. 16:13, here also); wherever we are, in the city or in the desert, in the house or in the field, in the shop or in the street, we may keep up our intercourse with Heaven if it be not our own fault....

...Note, The more we see of God the more cause we see for holy trembling and blushing before him. Those to whom God is pleased to manifest himself are thereby laid, and kept, very low in their own eyes, and see cause to fear even the Lord and his goodness, (Hos. 3:5). He said..., "The appearance of God in this place is never to be thought of, but with a holy awe and reverence. I shall have a respect for this place, and remember it by this token, as long as I live:" not that he thought the place itself any nearer the divine visions than other places; but what he saw there at this time was, as it were, the house of God, the residence of the divine Majesty, and the gate of heaven, that is, the general rendezvous of the inhabitants of the upper world, as the meetings of a city were in their gates; or the angels ascending and descending were like travellers passing and re-passing through the gates of a city.[2]

Jacob experienced an authentic heavenly encounter, and it changed him overnight. Now he was humbled by a holy awe; his stony sleeping place had become a tabernacle for the glory of God, his pillow an altar of remembrance.

God Does It Again—and Again!

Jacob's experience is unique in all of history. That being said, let me rush to say that *Jacob's ladder keeps coming down* from heaven. Why do I say that? Because of the testimonies of a lot of people. The true stories in this book are only a small sampling of the number of "ladders" that have come down from heaven into the lives of ordinary people like you and me. Look at these examples.

Angels visit orphans in China

Before he was forced to leave China by the revolution in 1949, missionary H. A. Baker worked among the beggar orphan children of southwest China. The Holy Spirit fell in an unprecedented way in the orphanage that he and his wife founded in Yunnanfu (now known as Kunming), Yunnan Province—Adullam Home. He recorded what happened in a now-classic book called *Visions Beyond the Veil.* (H. A. Baker is the grandfather of Rolland Baker, who today, with his wife, Heidi, is working with the poor in Mozambique, Africa.)

The children who lived at Adullam Home were mostly boys aged six to about eighteen who had been uneducated and wild and who had learned to survive on the streets. At the home, they were introduced to the Bible and taught to live in a new way. But that's not all. Heaven came to Earth, the children were often transported to the heavenly city to be entertained by angels, and their earthly caretakers were taken by as much delighted surprise as the children were. The children discovered the meaning of the scripture, "But you have come to Mount Zion, to the heavenly Jerusalem, the city of the living God. You have come to thousands upon thousands of angels in joyful assembly" (Heb. 12:22, NIV).

Baker relates: "These happy angels were not only at the gates, they were everywhere. They were always ready to escort the children wherever they wanted to go....Often in these experiences with the angels our children were given harps and taught to play them and sing as the angels did. They were also taught how to blow the trumpets, as well as much more about the music and language of heaven."[3]

As the Bakers watched, the children who were swept up into the angelic realm acted out with their bodies what they were experiencing with their spirits in heaven:

> When we saw the children, with closed eyes, all dancing around the room in rhythm, we discovered that in their vision they were dancing with the angels in heaven and keeping time with the heavenly music. When we saw them apparently blowing a trumpet or going through the motions of playing a harp, we found that in the

vision they were joining the heavenly orchestra praising the King. We could not see the heavenly harps or trumpets; we could not see the angels' joyful dance or hear their song; we could only hear the children singing heavenly songs. It was a daily occurrence to find a child, lying comfortably on some pine needles in a corner on his own, going through the motions of playing a harp. Going up to him, we could hear him singing a new song we had never taught him. As we got nearer still, we would discover that the words were as strange to us as the tune. The singer was singing in the heavenly choir. His song was the song the angels taught him. The words of the song must have been in the language of angels. Seeing the children singing in this heavenly angelic choir was unforgettable.

Sometimes several of them…would decide to play and sing together. With closed eyes…three or four of them would go off by themselves. If we were nearby we would hear them consult about who would play the trumpet and who would sing. After all was decided and everybody was ready, the heavenly songs began. The trumpeters held their hands up in front of them and blew as if they were blowing trumpets. The harpists both played and sang, while those without instruments joined in the singing. In these cases they always sang in languages we did not understand, unless by mutual agreement they decided to sing one of those hymns they "used to sing down on earth." In that case they sang in Chinese….

…Soon after entering the gates of the city the children were taken by the angels to "go and see Jesus." We could hear them talking about "going to see Jesus" and watched as in the vision they approached the throne of Christ. When they came into His wonderful presence they stood reverently gazing with love and devotion at the Lord of all creation, who was also their Saviour. First of all they thanked Him, and then clasping their hands in front of them they bowed low before Him in respect and loving adoration.[4]

Baker goes on to draw scriptural connections with these experiences. He noted that the children talked about angels whenever they were experiencing the power of the Holy Spirit at the same time.[5] He found scriptures that supported the idea that angels are involved in such experiences, such as the following description of John's experience:

The revelation of Jesus Christ, which God gave him to show his servants what must soon take place. He made it known by sending his angel to his servant John....

...On the Lord's Day I was in the Spirit, and I heard behind me a loud voice like a trumpet, which said: "Write on a scroll what you see and send it to the seven churches: to Ephesus, Smyrna, Pergamum, Thyatira, Sardis, Philadelphia and Laodicea."

I turned around to see the voice that was speaking to me. And when I turned I saw seven golden lampstands, and among the lampstands was someone "like a son of man," dressed in a robe reaching down to his feet and with a golden sash around his chest....

When I saw him, I fell at his feet as though dead. Then he placed his right hand on me and said: "Do not be afraid. I am the First and the Last. I am the Living One; I was dead, and behold I am alive for ever and ever! And I hold the keys of death and Hades.

"Write, therefore, what you have seen, what is now and what will take place later....

"To the angel of the church in Ephesus write..."

—Revelation 1:1, 10–13, 17–19; 2:1, NIV

You might recall the scripture that indicates that each true church has a special angel assigned to it (Rev. 1:20). Each person who is saved also receives ongoing ministry from at least one assigned angel:

Are not all angels ministering spirits sent to serve those who will inherit salvation?

—Hebrews 1:14, NIV

"You're out of your mind," they told her [the servant girl Rhoda]. When she kept insisting that it was so [that Peter was at the door], they said, "It must be his angel."

—Acts 12:15, NIV

[Jesus said,] "See that you do not look down on one of these little ones. For I tell you that their angels in heaven always see the face of my Father in heaven."

—Matthew 18:10, NIV

We can depend on angels to help us in every situation, especially when somebody is praying.

A Czech pastor's experience

A pastor named Evald Ruffy told me what happened to him in 1991 when he was in a coma. I have verified with him that these details are accurate.[6]

At the time, he was a pastor in the city of Liberec, in what was then called Czechoslovakia (now the Czech Republic). He was the pastor of a Moravian congregation that was growing rapidly, and he was working so hard that he had a heart attack in Sweden, where he had gone to minister.

He was lying in a coma in a hospital bed in Sweden, with his wife at his bedside praying for him, along with his best friend and associate pastor, Peter. As Evald said, "Peter carried with him the prayers of the saints. He was the point of the spear, and they were the shaft." Everyone was concerned because there were no signs of life.

As it turns out, Evald had actually escaped for three days. He had been privileged to tour heaven. For those three days, he forgot that he was a husband, a father, and a pastor whose work was not yet complete. He just enjoyed God and the sights.

Evald was shown ten specific things, one of which was like an Ezekiel experience. In that experience, he seemed to be standing almost between heaven and Earth, and he could see Central Europe. Dark clouds covered it. Then he saw white lights were going up and down, up and down through the black clouds, breaking them up. Evald turned to his heavenly guide and asked, "What is this?"

His interpreter responded, "Oh, those dark clouds, those are the territorial spirits of darkness that have been resting over Central Europe."

"Well, what are those white lights?" Evald asked.

"Oh, those are the angels. They are breaking up the powers of darkness."

Evald asked one more question: "How does this happen that the angels are released to break up the powers of darkness?"

The interpreter, the guide of the Holy Spirit, said, "This too happens in answer to the prayers of the saints."

Here we see it again—angels descending to Earth, sent by God in response to prayers, and ascending when they have finished each task. Jacob's ladder keeps on coming down.

Restoring heavenly inheritances

You may have heard of Shawn Bolz, a young man who was one of my students some years ago when I worked with Grace Training Center in Kansas City. Shawn is a prophetic brother who is now a popular speaker and author. In his book *Keys to Heaven's Economy: An Angelic Visitation from the Minister of Finance*, Shawn tells what happened to him one summer morning:

> All the sun's intensity seemed to blaze through my bedroom window that morning of July 5, 2001. The sun's rising was so brilliant that I turned the other way to avoid it, but as I rolled over, mirrors reflected the light straight into my eyes. Blinded from both sides, I sat up, squinted, and looked down at the edge of my bed. What I saw stunned me: A man stood there watching me.
>
> I studied him for a few seconds and realized he was not a human being but an angel who carried the very atmosphere of Heaven—and not just any angel, but one of Heaven's great angelic beings. I had never had an experience quite like this, and the fear of the Lord gripped my heart.
>
> Although this angel carried an air of nobility, he was dressed rather humbly in a brown robe that looked like burlap. It was covered with pockets. Beneath the robe was another garment that appeared translucent and alive, much like living light.

The angel was approximately six feet tall with brown hair and piercing hazel eyes, which I wanted to avoid looking into because I was frightened by the intensity of the love and authority they conveyed. At the same time, I couldn't seem to take away my gaze—we were totally eye-locked. His face radiated both compassion and authority. Suddenly, I understood why John the Beloved had become confused and worshipped an angel who had appeared to him (Revelation 19:10), because angels foreshadow God's radiant and luminous appearance.

Before I could say anything, the Lord's audible voice filled the room, introducing the angel standing before me: "Welcome, the Minister of Finance of the Kingdom."

The sound was both a trumpet and a voice in one. Waves of the Lord's presence rippled through me. Later, I found out that a young boy in the next room had been awakened and terrified by the audible voice of God....

Immediately, I knew this angel had command over all the finances and resources that heavenly authority calls forth from earth. These resources have only one purpose: to bring Jesus His full reward and inheritance in our age.[7]

The noble angel walked around the foot of Shawn's bed, drawing closer to him in order to show him a series of visions. Shawn writes that the angel was so quiet he could hear his own heart pounding in his chest.

Then the angel began to reach into the pockets of his robe, and, at a supernaturally fast speed, he began to pull out more than a hundred *keys* and put them all onto a kind of a key chain—"house keys, car keys, office keys, hotel room keys, card keys, window keys, bank keys, safety deposit keys, and many other different types. I even saw some futuristic keys that have not been used yet."[8]

The Minister of Finance angel pressed the whole key chain into Shawn's chest and deep into his spirit. "I was stunned....It was like cinematic special effects....I felt an electric shock as [the angel's hands] touched me....Instantly, I had the impression that I was not alone in this experience. I represented many believers who were receiving keys from Heaven to prepare the way of the Lord."[9]

Shawn had a series of visions, all of which he describes in detail in his book. Then, "after this series of visions, the Minister of Finance looked upward, and as I followed his gaze, he flew up and out of the room. My bedroom ceiling disappeared and Heaven opened over me. As I gazed into the open Heavens, I saw awesome visions."[10]

This was just the beginning for Shawn Bolz, and it is just the beginning for us. Jacob's ladder...open heavens...God's kingdom coming to Earth.

Going Higher Up

We are not alone. We have a *lot* more angelic company than we realize most of the time. Having just a glimpse of the angelic host shows us that we are not alone.

Over the centuries, people have wondered how many angels must exist. Of course, there is no firm answer to this question, anymore than there is a firm answer to how many stars are in the sky, how many grains of sand are on the seashores of the world, or even how many human beings have ever existed on Planet Earth. Pascal Parente, in his book *Beyond Space,* considers this question:

> The exact number of Angels that inhabit the heavenly Jerusalem has not been revealed. To try to determine their number must appear like an idle question, since man has not been able even to determine the exact number of stars. The vast number of stars, each one a sun in itself, is awe-inspiring and quite beyond our powers of comprehension. Until now, no known mechanical device has been able to even remotely suggest the magnitude of this visible universe. What must be the magnitude, the splendor, and glory of the invisible, immutable Angelic part of the universe? What the vastness of the spirit world, the number of those splendors that decorate the heavenly home, the House of God, if the house of man, our earth, is surrounded by such an infinity of stars? Who has ever been able to

count all the men and women who have inhabited this earth from the beginning to the present time?[11]

So many unanswerable questions! We inhabit a mere corner of reality. And yet, sometimes God opens a portal to heaven so we can catch a glimpse behind the scenes.

Before the throne of God, the prophet Daniel saw: "Thousands upon thousands attended him; ten thousand times ten thousand stood before him" (Dan. 7:10, NIV). That's not a definite number. It's just a wild estimation of the myriads and multitudes of angels Daniel saw in his vision.

Isaiah wrote:

> I saw the Lord seated on a throne, high and exalted, and the train of his robe filled the temple. Above him were seraphs, each with six wings: With two wings they covered their faces, with two they covered their feet, and with two they were flying. And they were calling to one another:
>
> "Holy, holy, holy is the LORD Almighty;
> the whole earth is full of his glory."
>
> —Isaiah 6:1–3, NIV

The apostle John recorded, "Then I looked and heard the voice of many angels, numbering thousands upon thousands, and ten thousand times ten thousand. They encircled the throne and the living creatures and the elders" (Rev. 5:11, NIV).

You will find angels at work throughout both the Old and New Testaments; more than three hundred times, angels are mentioned or referenced. They are everywhere, uncountable myriads of them:

> Praise Him, all His angels; Praise Him, all His hosts!
>
> —Psalm 148:2

[Jesus said,] "Or do you think that I cannot appeal to My Father, and He will at once put at My disposal more than twelve legions of angels?"

—Matthew 26:53

The chariots of God are myriads, thousands upon thousands.

—Psalm 68:17

This is the blessing that Moses the man of God pronounced on the Israelites before his death. He said: "The LORD came from Sinai and dawned over them from Seir; he shone forth from Mount Paran. He came with myriads of holy ones from the south, from his mountain slopes."

—Deuteronomy 33:1–2, NIV

We are not alone. When we pray, "Thy kingdom come, Thy will be done on earth as it is in heaven," we are welcoming heaven's hosts to come and join us, aid us, and strengthen us. They're ready to come.

So, Lord, we welcome Your angels, Your messengers. We welcome them however they may come, whether in fire or wind or without any sound at all. We say, as Your people have said through all the ages, "We need help from heaven." We need to be strengthened. We call forth once again for Jacob's ladder to come down into our earth realm. In the name of Jesus, amen.

Come, Thou Fount of ev'ry blessing,
Tune my heart to sing Thy grace;
Streams of mercy, never ceasing,
Call for songs of loudest praise.
Teach me some melodious sonnet,
Sung by flaming tongues above.
Praise the mount! I'm fixed upon it,
Mount of Thy redeeming love.[1]

TWO

My Personal
Angelic Encounters

The apostle Luke describes how the priest Zacharias, after he had been chosen to enter the holy place to burn incense, met an angel there, Gabriel himself. Probably an angelic encounter was about the last thing Zacharias expected. He was just going about his duty. It was special to be chosen for that duty, but not usually *that* special:

In the days of Herod, king of Judea, there was a priest named Zacharias, of the division of Abijah; and he had a wife from the daughters of Aaron, and her name was Elizabeth.

They were both righteous in the sight of God, walking blamelessly in all the commandments and requirements of the Lord. But they had no child, because Elizabeth was barren, and they were both advanced in years.

Now it happened that while he was performing his priestly service before God in the appointed order of his division, according to the custom of the priestly office, he was chosen by lot to enter the temple of the Lord and burn incense. And the whole multitude of the people were in prayer outside at the hour of the incense offering.

And an angel of the Lord appeared to him, standing to the right of the altar of incense. Zacharias was troubled when he saw the angel, and fear gripped him. But the angel said to him, "Do not be afraid, Zacharias, for your petition has been heard, and your wife Elizabeth will bear you a son, and you will give him the name John....It is he who will go as a forerunner before Him in the spirit and power of Elijah, to turn the hearts of the fathers back to the children, and the disobedient to the attitude of the righteous, so as to make ready a people prepared for the Lord."...

The angel...said to him, "I am Gabriel, who stands in the presence of God, and I have been sent to speak to you and to bring you this good news."

—Luke 1:5–13, 17, 19

Notice what the angel said (v. 13)—"your petition has been heard." Zacharias and Elizabeth, and probably their relatives and other faithful people, had been praying and interceding and petitioning God for a long, long time. In essence, they had filled up a bowl in heaven with their prayers. They had prayed for a child, and they had also prayed for Messiah to come to save Israel. Now the heavenly bowl was full to the brim. It was time. God was turning it over, pouring it out on faithful Zacharias and Elizabeth. Elizabeth, who had been barren and who had all but given up on motherhood, conceived. Nine months later, she gave birth to John the Baptist, cousin of Jesus, who was born about six months later. John, as we all know, was the forerunner for his cousin, the Messiah.

Obviously, this is a one-of-a-kind event. But it teaches us something about angels, something that applies to our own lives and to many circumstances all over the world throughout the centuries. What it teaches us is this: *prayers release God's power, and God often sends His angels to bring His powerful response to faithful prayers.* That's what happened to Zacharias, and it still happens for us today.

To give you some examples of what I mean, I want to remain in storytelling mode for another chapter in order to share more personal angelic encounters.

"It's Time to Begin"

In the early 1980s, God used the prophet Bob Jones to give a word to Mike Bickle in Kansas City. The word was a directive one: if some "forerunners" would unite to pray for ten years—morning, noon, and night—God would cause something new to break forth on the global scene for the body of Christ. So Mike and company prayed. I was involved with many of those prayer gatherings. For ten years—morning, noon, and night—forerunner prayer went up.

At the end of those ten years, in early 1994, something new definitely broke out, and it's still breaking out in the body of Christ. It goes by various names: "The Renewal," "The Refreshing," "The Father's Blessing," and more. It involves the presence of God manifested in ways that people had never before experienced on such a scale. All over the world, God began to show up when groups of people were worshiping Him in the Spirit, releasing signs and wonders and all sorts of amazing experiences. The incense of the prayers of the saints had gone up and up, and finally it was time for God's power to come down. (After all, "What goes up must come down.")

In the springtime of that same year, I was in Indianapolis, Indiana, ministering at a gathering called "City of Destiny." While I was there, I was sleeping in a second-floor bedroom of a house. Suddenly I was awakened by the sound of a trumpet, although it was more of a shofar sound, and by the voice of the Lord coming through an angel.

I sat up in bed, wide-awake. The room was thick with the manifest presence of God. The very atmosphere conveyed the sense of *destiny*. (When angels cross over from the eternal realm to the temporal one and bring with them the manifest presence of God, there can be different "flavors" to the way the presence feels. This time God's presence felt like destiny.) This sense of God's presence and this sense of destiny lasted for maybe twenty minutes, while I just sat there in the bed, not saying a word. Then, at the end of my bed, I saw an angel.

I don't know how tall this angel was, because the angel wasn't in the appearance of a man. This angel looked more like a "typical" angel, if there is such a thing, covered with glowing, feathery, satiny, radiant white garments. Its wings were held to its sides, and they were enormous. I couldn't say a word. I didn't want to say a word. I was speechless because of the incredible radiant presence in the room and the fear of the Lord and the tangible sense of destiny. I don't know what kind of angel this was, but I know it was some kind of a covering angel or covering cherub, maybe even an archangel—some kind that has authority over other angels. I could tell that much by what happened next.

The angel opened up its wings. I don't know how many wings it had, at least two. Then a hand like a man's hand proceeded out from under the wings. It reminded me of scriptural descriptions of the seraphim. In the angel's hand was a green measuring cup, an incredibly green measuring cup. I associate the color green as the color of the Levites, the priests, who are the ones who intercede. And green could also be interpreted to mean new life.

In this cup was fresh oil. And then for the next twenty minutes, I watched this angel dispatch scores of other angels, hundreds, maybe even thousands of them. They were just taking off as fast as they could— *swoosh! Swoosh! Swoosh!* They were being released to go out over the whole world. These angels carried bottles of fresh oil, and they carried bottles of new wine. I was amazed.

Over in the corner of the room, I saw a large bottle of oil perhaps eighteen inches tall. The bottle was labeled "Crisco." For a split second, I allowed my unspiritual thoughts to rise up and wonder, "Oh, *why* does the prophetic always have to be so parabolic?" Then immediately I understood the meaning. "Oh, of course! It's Crisco. Cris—Jesus Christ." The Greek word is *Christos*, which means "the Anointed One." "And the 'co'—the anointing is not being released for one person, but for a *company*." I understood it—fresh oil was being released through the messengers of Jesus Christ to the company of the body of Christ.

As these angels were going out, *swoosh, swoosh*, all over the earth, I understood the word that had been spoken aloud at the first sound of the trumpet-shofar. The word I had heard was, "It's time to begin!" It was time to begin a new outpouring. It was time to cross a new threshold in church history. We had the Jesus movement thirty years before, and now it was time to begin something new.

It's true that something new has been happening in the dozen or so years since then. Something definite did begin then, and angels were (and are) a vital part of it—in response to the Spirit-inspired, fervent prayers of the people of God.

An Angel Leads the Way in Minsk

You will probably remember the disaster that happened in 1986 at the nuclear power plant in Chernobyl in the former USSR (now Ukraine). The zone of damaging radioactive contamination was still spreading when I traveled to Minsk, Belarus, to serve as a prophetic intercessor for a festival outreach for Jewish people. I had gone there with my two friends, David Fitzpatrick and Richard Glickstein, with whom I had prayed a lot in New York City and other places in the United States.

After we had pretty much completed our assignment as intercessors for the event, we all felt we had an additional assignment to complete—to intervene in prayer for the protection of the city, especially the children, against what was being called "Chernobyl Disease." It was expected to contaminate the river that runs through Minsk, and if it did, the ramifications for the people would be devastating. We had reconnoitered a bit, and we had found a particular place in the city where a bridge crossed the river by some old Communist monuments. We felt that was where we should gather to pray.

So the three of us, who were staying in different rooms on different floors of the hotel, met up late one night to go visit the place we had scouted out during the daytime. We met up on the elevator, and another man happened to join us. When we got out, he got out with us, and he followed us out to the street.

Now, at first we thought we knew where we were going. We had been there in the daylight. But now, not only was it dark, but also the subway system, which was immense and complex, was only functioning in a limited way at night. We didn't know how to get to where we thought we were supposed to go. So we just walked down the steps to the train tracks. We got on a train that felt to us like the right one. The fourth man got on with us. He looked like a typical Russian man. He said nothing to us.

We got off the train when it stopped, but now we were really lost. We couldn't even remember which side of the tracks to stand on next.

Then the man came up alongside us and said, in English, "Come, stand over here!" He brought us from one side of the tracks to the other side, where we stood and waited for the next train. When it came, he stopped it and said, "Get on here." We looked at each other and decided we didn't know anything better to do, so we got on. That train whisked us away, and when it came to a stop, we got off again. Of course, we still didn't know what to do. Again we crossed over to the other side of the tracks, and again, when the next train showed up, the man said, "You get on here!" What else could we do? We got on again, with this Russian-looking man we didn't know, who happened to be able to speak English. (In Minsk, Belarus, there weren't very many people who spoke English!)

We got off again, this time in what looked like a major interchange, with a lot of different exits. We were walking, totally lost. The man got off with us and walked with us. Then he pointed to an exit and said to us, "Your assignment rests right out here." We walked up the steps and found ourselves at the exact spot that we were looking for! But now the man wasn't with us. We turned and looked for him. In a split second, I darted back down the stairs to look for him. Of course, I could not find him. He was gone. Surely, our "Russian" guide was an angel.

So we completed our assignment, which involved going down the street to the bridge over the river. We picked up a big tree limb along the way that just "happened" to be there, remembering Jeremiah 23:5, the "righteous Branch." And we took it down to the river to do a prophetic act that was similar to what Moses did in Exodus 15, when he took a stick and put it into the bitter water, and it was made sweet. We threw the branch into the river and declared that the radiation would not come into this river, that the "bitter water would be made sweet."

Afterwards, we found out that the radiation had never gotten into the city via the river. We had completed our assignment, with the very important help of an angel.

Warrior Angels and Tyler's Birth

In the middle of the summer of 1988, an important set of prayer gatherings occurred in Evian, France, and in Berlin, Germany. This was before the Berlin wall came down. Instead of being in Europe attending the gatherings, I was at home with Michal Ann and our two young children because Michal Ann was nine months pregnant with our third child.

Nine and a half months earlier, we had had an extraordinary visitation from three angels. That night, at precisely 2:34 a.m., a wind had blown through the closed bedroom window and through our bedroom. It had blown open the bedroom door, gusted down the hallway, turned around, and had come back through the door, slamming it shut. And then it went back out through the same closed window. ("He makes his angels winds..." [Heb. 1:7, NIV].) Michal Ann and I had been awakened instantly, sitting up in bed together with the wind blowing through our bedroom.

Then, in fast succession, we both had seen and heard and sensed a number of things, some of them together and some of them separately. Michal Ann sensed a broad stretch of angel wings. I heard the voice of the Lord. We both sensed the Holy Spirit hovering over our bed, up by the ceiling.

And then an angel had appeared sort of from the top down, glistening, and the terror of God filled the room. At the end of our bed, there stood a man, dressed in a military uniform—white pants, long red coat, triangular-shaped hat, with a musket by his side. He said nothing; he just stared at us. Then he disappeared, and another one swooped in and stood in the same spot. This one was also in a military uniform, a dark blue outfit with middle buttons down the coat and a different type of hat. His gun, I remember, had a bayonet on the end. He didn't say anything, either, and then he took off. Shortly after he left, I recognized that these two were messengers, or symbols, of two wars that occurred on American soil—the Revolutionary War and the Civil War.

Just as suddenly as the other two, a third angel appeared. This one was modern looking, and he was dressed in a modern way—I don't know what branch of the military his uniform represents—and yet it felt futuristic. His presence carried great authority. Inside myself, I thought, "You look like you could be a relative of mine." I somehow knew that just as the first two represented two wars that had been fought on American soil, this angel could be a messenger of a future war that could be fought on this soil. Then, instead of remaining silent as the others had done, this one spoke. He said, "It's time for Tyler Hamilton." The clock turned to 3:00, and he left. The appearance of the three soldier angels and some subsequent revelations from God have carried major ramifications, but for the purposes of this chapter, I want to share the part about Tyler.

Fast forward to nine and a half months later. In the wee hours of July 7, Michal Ann was in bed, but I was up praying in our living room. I was thinking about the gatherings in Europe, and I was engaged in acts of identificational repentance because of my Goll (German) ancestral line, confessing generational sins as Daniel did in Daniel 9 and 10, especially repenting for what the Germans had done against the Jewish people and how the church had not raised her voice during the Holocaust of World War II.

Suddenly, at 1:17 a.m., this same "modern" warrior angel appeared in the doorway of our living room. He said, "It's time for Tyler Hamilton to come forth. You must go and lay hands upon your wife and call him forth."

So I got up and walked into the bedroom. I told my wife, "Tyler's angel has just come"—not that I understood exactly what that meant. I just remembered that nine and a half months earlier, I'd said, "You look like you could be a relative of mine," and I had felt that there was a warrior anointing on our third child. I knew that there are yet many more pages to be written about the wars of the Lord and about our engagement in fighting some of the battles, and I felt that our son would play a role in future spiritual combat.

I told Michal Ann that the angel had told me to lay hands on her and call him forth. She said, "Well, just do it!" So I laid my hands on her protruding stomach and said, "Tyler Hamilton, this is the voice of your father speaking. Your angel has just come and said that I must lay hands on your mother to call you forth. Listen and obey. This is your father speaking. The time has come. Come forth!" My wife started having contractions, and a few hours later, on July 7, 1988, Tyler Hamilton was born.

Why did angels have to get involved in this birth? I don't really know. That's the way it always goes. An angelic encounter occurs, often when it is least expected, and it is awesome. I can never comprehend more than a fraction of what's going on; I just try to keep up with whatever God sends my way. Yes, as terrifying as an angelic encounter can sometimes be, I want more of them. Every time it happens, I feel I'm getting another glimpse of our heavenly home, where we'll all be able to see angels all the time.

One Thing

The one thing that ties all angel stories together is God. When we experience an angelic visitation, whether or not it's a spectacular, almost-indescribable one, we are receiving a touch from God. When we see or hear or feel one of His angels, God is bringing His kingdom to Earth in one more way.

He wants to "love on" His people. His faithful, strong angels are His messengers of love.

> *Thank You, Father, for giving us personal experiences*
> *with Your angels. Truly You send the heavenly host to*
> *work with us, Your weak, earthbound servants. I ask that*
> *You will use these true stories as an avenue of inspira-*
> *tion for others. May these accounts show clearly how close*
> *heaven is to us, how approachable, how available,*
> *and how real. Amen.*

Teach me to love Thee as Thine angels love,
One holy passion filling all my frame;
The kindling of the heav'n-descended Dove,
My heart an altar, and Thy love the flame.[1]

THREE

Invaded!

(by Michal Ann Goll)

I was exhausted, but I just couldn't sleep off my tiredness—at least not at night.

Anyway, I didn't really *want* to sleep straight through the night, because that's when the angels were visiting me! Every night for about nine weeks they would come to my bedroom, particularly when Jim (as I refer to him) was out of town and I was home alone with our four children, who were young at the time. Probably I will never fully understand why I had such an intense season of angelic encounters, although I came away from those weeks with quite a few clear ideas about the reasons (which I will mention throughout this chapter). Here's the story of what happened.

Angel in a Lightning Bolt

Psalm 97 has this line: "His lightning lights up the world; the earth sees and trembles" (Ps. 97:4, NIV). Many people believe—and now I'm one of them—that sometimes angels come to us in the midst of actual lightning or wind or both.

25

We were living in Missouri, and on this particular night in October of 1992, there was a great windstorm with thunder and lightning. Jim had arrived home late, after teaching a night class at Grace Training Center in Kansas City. It happened to be the Day of Atonement, and he knew that often God speaks to His people on that day, so he had led the class in a time of consecration to God, during which the class had felt the supernatural wind of the Spirit and the solemn presence of the Lord in the auditorium. Giving his assistant Chris Berglund a ride home, Jim had commented to him that God was going to come and speak that night.

He dropped Chris off and came on home. Coming into our bedroom in the dark, he found our youngest son, Tyler, who had been frightened by the storm, sound asleep on the floor next to his side of the bed. He slipped into bed next to me and fell asleep himself.

Suddenly, a lightning bolt struck the backyard, and light burst in through the bedroom window. Jim woke up instantly, but I didn't. A man was standing at the end of our bed! The atmosphere became saturated with the presence of the terror of God, and Jim lay there trembling for one full minute, staring at this man, who was dressed in brown trousers and looking right at him.

Exactly as the readout of the digital clock changed to twelve o'clock midnight, the angel spoke. He said, "Watch your wife. I'm about to speak to her," and he disappeared. At the same time, the manifest presence of God increased in the room, and Jim noticed a supernatural light glowing over our bedroom dresser. Jim simply said, "Ann, an angel has just come."

Fully awake

All he had to say was "Ann..." and I was instantly awake. We'd had other experiences with angels visiting us in the night, and immediately I knew that it was about to happen again. Evidently, this encounter was meant for me alone, because—unbelievably—James just rolled over and fell asleep. (We have decided that the angel wanted Jim to witness this manifestation, but not the entire encounter. So it must have been a supernatural sleep that the Lord took him into.)

There I lay, on my stomach, with the terror of God thick in the room. I wanted to hide, but all I could do was wait for something to happen. I gathered all of my courage and prayed that I'd be brave enough to withstand whatever was about to happen. I really wanted God to come and to give me everything He wanted to impart to me, and I didn't want to interfere with the moment. But I was terrified!

What happened next was surprisingly pleasant. My ears had been hurting for several days. Suddenly I began to feel warm, soothing oil being poured into my left ear. (I was lying on my right ear.) It felt wonderful. I glanced at the clock, and it was 1:34 in the morning. I believe that time corresponds with Psalm 134:1, which reads, "Behold, bless ye the Lord, all ye servants of the Lord, which by night stand in the house of the Lord" (kjv).

Gathering my courage, I turned my head over. The same thing started happening to my right ear. It felt so good. Then more things began to happen.

Pressure started building up in my head. It got stronger and stronger. I didn't know what in the world was going on. Just when I thought I couldn't take it anymore, the pressure subsided, only to start building against my back. I felt like somebody had placed a board on my back and was pushing me into the bed. It squeezed the breath right out of me, and I thought I must have been making some kind of a loud noise, but Jim didn't wake up, so maybe I didn't. I also felt like the finger of God was working its way into my chest, reworking and rearranging my insides. It was very intense.

Finally, the pushing eased up, and I glanced at the clock again. Exactly thirty minutes had passed. It read "2:04," which later led me to read Proverbs 2:4 (including verse 5): "If you seek [Wisdom] as for silver and search for skillful and godly Wisdom as for hidden treasures, then you will understand the reverent and worshipful fear of the Lord and find the knowledge of [our omniscient] God" (amp).

After that, I felt like I was being pulled away from Jim's side while still on the bed. Afraid, I reached out my arm toward him, but somehow I couldn't touch him. Something seemed to be holding my arm back. I don't think my body actually moved, but it *felt* like I was being pulled. The whole thing was really bizarre, to the point that I really began to wonder if it was God.

Fully undone

This series of experiences left me completely undone. I literally did not know if I was still alive or not, and I actually put my fingers up to my neck to see if I had a pulse. I wondered if my hair had turned white or if my face looked different. My skin was kind of cold and clammy. Later, when Jim woke up, he said my lips were purple. The blanket felt real thin. I wanted to hide. I could do nothing to relieve my feeling of absolute vulnerability. I felt so *human* and fleshly. Never before or since have I had such an unnerving experience.

For the rest of the night, I lay there awake. Jim and I would talk a bit, then he'd fall back asleep, then he'd wake up, and we'd talk a bit more. We asked the Lord to confirm that this whole thing was from Him by giving dreams to our children. At one point, I was taken up in my spirit for about thirty minutes, and I could look down and see my body in the bed. I saw other things, including a white warhorse, and I heard things. Little did I know that this was just the first night of a long season of these angelic visitations.

The light kept flickering over our dresser (where Jim had left a letter from a seer prophet that concerned God's call on our lives) until seven o'clock in the morning—I was awake the whole night, absolutely riveted, and basically scared out of my mind. Finally, after 7:00 a.m., though, I dropped off to sleep for a while.

Later in the morning, when Jim and I woke up again, there was little Tyler standing by Jim's side of the bed like a tin soldier. He said, "Daddy, I just had a dream that an angel came and visited our house last night." His older brother Justin had been sleeping in his bed in the room directly above ours, and he reported that he'd had a dream in which someone took him into a barn to see a white horse—the same white warhorse that I had seen. There was the confirmation we had asked for.

Somehow, there was grace to get through the daylight hours. We were supposed to homeschool, but no way was it a normal day. I felt like there was a whole encampment of angels in the house. There was such an awesome presence of God's glory throughout every room. Every time I walked into a room, I didn't know what or whom I was going to see. I just walked around feeling a kind of strange expectation. I'd think, "Oh, yeah—I need to fix breakfast for the kids....Oh, yeah, I need to fix GraceAnn's hair." (I even forgot how to do that at one point.) Once, I was sitting on the couch and GraceAnn, who was five at the time, walked up behind me and touched me. I nearly jumped out of my skin!

Perspective From the Word

I found something in the Book of Job that helped me describe this experience:

> Now a thing was secretly brought to me, and my ear received a whisper of it. In thoughts from the visions of the night, when deep sleep falls on men, fear came upon me and trembling, which made all my bones shake.
>
> —Job 4:12–14, AMP

I remembered biblical accounts of angelic visitations, for example, what happened to the shepherds at Bethlehem the night Jesus was born. There's a *reason* they fell down. There's a reason John fell "like a dead man" (Rev. 1:17). There's a reason the angels are always saying, "Fear not." It's a fearful thing when God unzips His Superman suit a little and lets some of His glory shine out. Our mortal bodies just can't handle it, even a small taste.

With the help of a discerning friend, I began to realize that the different aspects of that first night had meaning for the broader body of Christ. It was as if I had entered into a prophetic intercessory experience that had implications for the church as a whole. For instance, the intense pressure in my head and the incredible pushing on my back represented God's desire to push fear and unbelief out of His bride. That's why I felt as if my heart had stopped. It was as if Jesus came and said, "I want to rearrange your heart. My own heart cries out for an exclusive relationship with you." That's why I couldn't hold on to Jim in the night; the Lord wanted me to cling to Him alone. The Lord was saying, "I am jealous after you with true jealousy, and I will not be satisfied to have a relationship with you through your husband, your pastor, or anyone else."

After the first night, more angelic visitations occurred. In fact, they occurred, to one degree or another, every night for weeks and weeks. I believe that the main reason the angels came was so that I could be closer to Jesus. I said as much to Him: "Lord, if these experiences don't draw me closer to You and don't reveal more of Yourself to me, then of what use are they?"

The Lord Jesus wants to enable the whole body of believers to have unimpeded communion with Him. He is coming to restore the earth. He's coming to push fear and unbelief out of His bride, the church. He's coming to open our ears so that we can hear like a disciple. As I learned, His angelic messengers are not always very quiet and gentle when they help us hear Him.

> The Lord God has given Me the tongue of disciples, that I may know how to sustain the weary one with a word. He awakens Me morning by morning, He awakens My ear to listen as a disciple. The Lord God has opened My ear; and I was not disobedient nor did I turn back. I gave My back to those who strike me.
>
> —Isaiah 50:4–6

Everything was different for a while. Instead of settling down for a night's sleep, I would gear up for the angels to come. They would wake me up by slapping my feet or slapping my shoulder. (Remember how the angel woke Peter up when he was in prison? "Suddenly an angel of the Lord appeared and a light shone in the cell. He struck Peter on the side and woke him up" [Acts 12:7, NIV].) It was as if they were saying, "Wake up! Wake up! You *can't* be asleep!"

I remember one Saturday morning. Jim was gone. (He had a grueling travel schedule much of that year.) All of a sudden, I became aware that someone had touched me on my left hand with two fingers. It was no normal touch; the instant I was touched, my hand was filled with energy and heat. Liquid fire flowed over to my right hand. It began to spread down to my feet. It coursed all through my body for about thirty minutes. I was just gyrating. Afterward, I turned on the light, and my hands were actually pink and a little swollen—and there was a white spot in the middle of my hand, right where I had been touched. These experiences were not comfortable.

Over and over, I would become too scared to handle it. I just felt like I wasn't going to live through it. I'd beg the Lord to ease up. "O Lord, I'm sorry, but I'm just going to ask You not to come. Please don't come. This is too intense." Then the next morning, I'd be frustrated with myself that I had been such a scaredy-cat. I'd tell the Lord, "I'm sorry about what I said in the night. I really want You to come. I really do." Then nighttime would come, and I'd get scared all over again. Finally, I thought I had figured out how to pray. I would say, "Lord, I want You to listen to the prayers of my strength. Don't listen to the prayers of my weakness. If tonight I tell You not to come, don't listen to me. I really do want You to come!"

But the Lord didn't want me to pray that way for very long. He simply said, "What do you want? I want to come and visit you. There are things that I want to give you. I promise that I'll never leave you or forsake you. But if you really don't want Me to come like this, then I will stop coming. I want you to stop praying like this. Stop vacillating. Decide once and for all what you really want. Then tell Me."

It took me three days to make up my mind, and I shed lots of tears. This was no small matter. The fear of the Lord is clean; it's not like the fear of an enemy, but it's terrifying just the same.

Finally, after three days of saying, "God, help me," I yielded. I told Him I really wanted Him to come and that I wasn't going to go back and forth anymore. I told Him I meant it, even if it meant I would die in the process. I told Him I had no place else to go for life and that I would leave my fears behind.

So He kept coming.

Night After Night

The angelic visitations would get really intense when Jim was out on the road. When he'd come home, they would be more subdued. I wanted him to have these experiences with me, but it was as if the Lord had reserved them mostly for me.

Every evening at about 9:00 p.m., God's presence would begin to intensify. It seemed to reach a peak by about 11:00 p.m., and then I would be awake until about 4:00 in the morning, night after night. During the day, God would give me grace, and He would give the kids grace, too. They would be all right when I'd fall asleep during the day. There were people who came in and helped me. It was a season of grace.

No two experiences were alike. The same night I had the liquid fire going through me, I remember dropping off to sleep after a few hours and beginning to dream. In the dream, I was carrying on a conversation with someone I know, and he was telling me something about a changing table (which had become a standard piece of furniture in our household full of small children in diapers). Then he was walking around my room inspecting the heat vents and talking to me about being susceptible to allergies. As the dream progressed, I began to realize that I was *hearing* this person as he walked around, because he had squeaky shoes. Then I began to realize that it was more like my dream was blending with reality, as dreams sometimes do, because I really was hearing somebody's squeaky shoes walking around my bedroom. He'd squeak into the bathroom, back into the room, walking around and talking with me about things. I heard him come around the bed. Finally, I opened my eyes, and here was this angel who looked just like the person in the dream. The dream and reality blended together. I felt as if I had been having this long conversation with the angel and that it was the same angel who had touched me on the hand earlier. I felt like I'd been trying to find him in the hours since then. He was transparent, but he had brown hair that came down below his chin. He was wearing glasses and brown clothes. I blurted out, "There you are! Hi! Why are you here?" Instantly, he vanished.

Night after night, strange and wonderful things would happen. Sometimes I would have sensations such as a bitter taste on the tip of my tongue or a burning on my lips. Sometimes my tongue would get hard or my ears would pop or my nose would open up. I knew that the Lord was telling me there would come a time when I would have "hard faith," when I would have to say bitter things that people might not want to receive.

One night, fireballs showed up by the ceiling. First, I became aware of flashes of heat coming down over me; then I saw a white fireball in the air, and it came down and hit me. I said "O Lord, do it again. I want You to come. I want You to come and visit me as much as You want to." I felt that the challenge from the Lord was to engage in what He was doing, to get every last drop out of what He wanted to release to me. Another fireball appeared. It was burning and rotating, like it was set, ready to go. I said, "Hit me! Hit me!" and it just flew toward me and exploded in my chest. Then I'd say, "I want another one! Another one!" And another one would appear up by the ceiling. The fire of God would be released inside of me, and I kept calling for more. As long as they kept showing up, I kept calling for more, until maybe twelve or fifteen of them had been released.

Jesus Himself

After a while, the Lord gave me a promise. He said, "Next time, not only will the angels come. Now Jesus Himself will come." That put everything into perspective.

I had been trying to journal everything, to keep track, which I believe the Lord wanted me to do. I wanted to understand it. But it became such a huge mountain of information! So much of it was in riddles.

Sometimes I didn't know how to write it down. I had so many questions that were not being answered at the time. I was getting more questions than I was getting answers. It seemed too much for me to process.

I would have dreams where I would hear Jesus singing, "Where is My bride, O My God?" He was longing for His bride to be ready for Him. He hears us sing our worship songs in church. We sing songs like "True Love," and *Jesus thinks we mean it!* We are arousing His love, but we don't know what we're doing. He's coming in response, and we don't even recognize it. We don't even know what He looks like. His heart is breaking, and He's asking, "Where is My bride, My God?"

My heart broke as I began to understand. He was shattering the hardness of my heart. He was making me able to hear what His heart was saying, and He was giving me an intercessory burden for the body of Christ. He was making me able to release His love to His bride and to release my love back to Him in prayer.

I didn't want to have experiences for the sake of having experiences. I didn't want to have them just so I could stand up in front of a group of people and say, "I've had angelic encounters." I wanted to have these experiences and be able to tell about them only for the sake of testifying about His love. I wanted to be able to impart some of His powerful love to others.

Bring me closer

My special season of angelic encounters ended after nine weeks. Toward the end, I felt like I could finally understand the Song of Solomon, because my heart was lovesick for the Lord. I knew that the season was changing, and I knew that what I had been experiencing was drawing to a close. I did everything I knew how to do to extend it. As frightening as it was, I did not want to have that chapter closed. I was lovesick. My heart was sick with love.

The Lord had allowed me to come into such a precious place in Him. He had shared such deep things with me. I couldn't imagine going back to regular routines, going to bed and sleeping all the way through the night, waking up thinking about what I was going to do that day, doing chores, going shopping for groceries, cooking dinner. I didn't want to go back to regular life. I was hungry for more of Him.

I came away from this time a changed person. No longer was I intimidated by other people. Now I had a new level of authority, even though I was not really aware of it. Jim said, "I don't know who you are or who you are becoming." I didn't know who I was either. He was shocked at the waves of authority he could feel when I even waved my hand toward him. The changes in me meant changes in our marriage. We had to make some adjustments.

Jim says he had thought he was married to the perfect wife, because I was totally compliant. And then when I got delivered from my fear of man, fear of rejection, and so forth, I became, in his words, a *lioness*. At first he thought he had liked me better before, when I was real quiet, but then we decided that God was remaking both of us into His image. As we were becoming more like Jesus, we'd have to continue to make more adjustments to each other. The important thing was to champion each other's journey—and to keep growing with Him.

Nine weeks was the equivalent of a nine-month gestation period. It was like a prophetic parable we walked through, because the Lord came to visit a bride (me) and He did things that showed us what He wants to do for His bride, the church. Just as the angel spoke to Jim and said, "Watch your wife. I'm about to speak to her," the message that's being spoken to the corporate church is, "Watch My bride. I'm about to speak to her."

Speak to us, Lord. Let that word come. Let the light shine. Angelic visitors, come and do God's bidding. May the light of His brilliance invade us and draw us into a greater intimacy with the Father, Son, and Holy Spirit. For the sake of Jesus Christ, our Savior, amen.

Angels, from the realms of glory,
Wing your flight o'er all the earth;
Ye who sang creation's story,
Now proclaim Messiah's birth:
Come and worship, come and worship,
Worship Christ, the newborn King![1]

FOUR

The Nature of These
Celestial Beings

Long before the church of Jesus Christ existed, even long before the Hebrew people existed, angels existed. Have you ever thought about that? God created the angels before He created human beings. They appear in the pages of both the Old and New Testaments, but were already alive and active long before the first book of the Bible was written.

Here's something else—no angel has ever died. There are myriads of them, and they perform many varied functions that we will be exploring in this chapter. Unlike us, angels are spirits, unlimited by space and time, unrestricted by bodies (although they can adopt various bodily forms). Angels can do things that amaze us.

The existence of angels has been acknowledged by people of many cultures and many religions throughout all of human civilization. In other words, the Judeo-Christian tradition cannot lay sole claim to them. But we can lay claim to having the closest association with them—because we are laboring together with them to bring the rule and reign of God's kingdom to the world.

Above all, angels exist to serve God. The very name *angel* denotes one of their functions, that of being a "messenger" of God. Here is how St. Augustine, influential preacher and father of the church, described angels in a sermon he preached in northern Africa at the end of the fourth century:

> "The Angels are spirits," says Saint Augustine, "but it is not because they are spirits that they are Angels. They become Angels when they are sent, for the name Angel refers to their office not to their nature. You ask the name of this nature, it is *spirit;* you ask its office, it is that of an Angel, (i.e., a messenger). In as far as he exists, an Angel is a spirit; in as far as he acts, he is an Angel." The word "angel" comes from a Greek word meaning "messenger." In the Scriptures of the Old Testament, the most frequently used [Hebrew] name to designate the Angels is *mal'akh,* which means messenger or legate.
>
> This generic name, "angel," does not reveal anything about the real nature of those celestial beings besides the fact that they are occasionally sent on a mission as messengers or legates of God to men.... They have been given the name of messengers from the most common duty and office they fulfill towards God's children here on earth. "And of the angels he saith, 'Who maketh his angels spirits, and his ministers a flame of fire'" [Heb. 1:7, KJV].[2]

Angels are not omniscient (all knowing), omnipresent (all present), or omnipotent (all powerful), as God is. But they are a lot more knowledgeable, available, and powerful than we are. In fact, a great deal of our experience of God's glorious, powerful presence depends on the angels who convey it and display it to us. Human beings exist to serve God, too, but we are much more limited in our supernatural reach than our co-workers the angels are.

More Definitions

Over the past few years, I have collected a number of books about angels, and I have ranged far and wide to include as much depth and breadth as possible. Here is a selection of what others have said about the nature of these celestial beings known as angels.

Martin Luther, German reformer (1483–1546): "An angel is a spiritual creature created by God without a body, for the service of Christendom and of the church."[3]

John Calvin, French reformer (1509–1564): "In Scripture, then, we uniformly read that angels are heavenly spirits, whose obedience and ministry God employs to execute all the purposes which he has decreed, and hence their name as being a kind of intermediate messengers to manifest his will to men. The names by which several of them are distinguished have reference to the same office. They are called hosts, because they surround their Prince as his court,—adorn and display his majesty,—like soldiers, have their eyes always turned to their leader's standard, and are so ready and prompt to execute his orders, that the moment he gives the nod, they prepare for, or rather are actually at work....As his government of the world is exercised and administered by them, they are called at one time Principalities, at another Powers, at another Dominions (Col. i:16; Eph. i:21)....

"...Angels are the ministers and dispensers of the divine bounty towards us. Accordingly, we are told how they watch for our safety, how they undertake our defence, direct our path, and take heed that no evil befall us....The protection of those whom he [the Lord] has undertaken to defend he has delegated to his angels....

"...Angels are ministering spirits (Heb. i:14); whose service God employs for the protection of his people, and by whose means he distributes his favours among men, and also executes other works."[4]

Contemporary, cross-traditional perspective. This is quoted from a book by Margaret Barker, a Methodist preacher who is the former president of the Society for Old Testament Study and a Hebrew scholar: "'Angel' means messenger, and humans experience angels primarily as messengers. But this is not what they 'are;' this is what they do. Angels exist to praise God and humans who experience their presence are being guided toward this universal hymn of praise. Mystics and seers have heard their song, and those who respond to the angels' message move inevitably toward the harmony the angels represent, the 'peace on earth' of the Bethlehem angels. By joining the song of the angels, human hearts and minds are connected to the power of the invisible creation, and their lives are renewed."[5]

Billy Graham, spokesman for twentieth-century evangelicalism: "Angels belong to a uniquely different dimension of creation that we, limited to the natural order, can scarcely comprehend. In this angelic domain the limitations are different from those God has imposed on our natural order. He has given angels higher knowledge, power and mobility than we.... They are God's messengers whose chief business is to carry out His orders in the world. He has given them an ambassadorial charge. He has designated and empowered them as holy deputies to perform works of righteousness. In this way they assist Him as their creator while He sovereignly controls the universe. So He has given them the capacity to bring His holy enterprises to a successful conclusion."[6]

Contemporary Jewish perspective: "In Judaism an angel is a spiritual entity in the service of God. Angels play a prominent role in Jewish thought throughout the centuries....

"A number of numinous creatures subordinate to God appear through the Hebrew Bible; the Malach (messenger/angel) is only one variety. Others, distinguished from angels proper, include Irinim (Watchers/ High Angels), Cherubim (Mighty Ones), Sarim (Princes), Seraphim (Fiery Ones), Chayyot ([Holy] Creatures), and Ofanim (Wheels). Collective terms for the full array of numina serving God include: Tzeva (Host), B'nei ha-Elohim or B'nai Elim (Sons of God), and Kedoshim (Holy Ones). They are constituted in an *Adat El,* a divine assembly (Ps. 82; Job 1). A select number of angels in the Bible (three to be precise) have names. They are Michael, Gabriel, and Satan.

"Angels can come in a wondrous variety of forms, although the Bible often neglects to give any description at all (Judges 6:11–14; Zech. 4). They appear humanoid in most Biblical accounts (Numbers 22) and as such are often indistinguishable from human beings (Gen. 18; 32:10–13; Joshua 5:13–15; Judges 13:1–5) but they also may manifest themselves as pillars of fire and cloud, or as a fire within a bush (Exod. 3). The Psalms characterize natural phenomenon, like lightning, as God's melachim (Ps. 104:4). Other divine creatures appear to be winged parts of

God's throne (Isa. 6) or of the divine chariot (Ezek. 1). The appearance of cherubim is well known enough to be artistically rendered on the Ark of the Covenant (Exod. 25). Perhaps the most ambiguous creature is the Malach Adonai, an angel that may or may not be a visible manifestation of God.

"Biblical angels fulfill a variety of functions, including conveying information to mortals, shielding, rescuing, and caring for Israelites, and smiting Israel's enemies."[7]

What a multifaceted lot God's angels are! It makes me want to burst forth in praise for the God whose kingdom is so endlessly awesome.

Let's let the quotes above launch us on our further discussion of the nature of angels.

Angels Described

Certainly you realize by now that most angels, if not all of them, do *not* resemble our contemporary, cutesy Christmas card and Valentine card renditions. Far from it. They often do seem to assume a human form, but it's not usually a feminine form or an infantile one. Angels are *not* all blonds, and they do not necessarily have wings. They are *much* more impressive than the "dumbed-down" version we have ended up with.

What do they look like, sound like, act like? How can we describe what we know about the nature of angels?

Angels are personal beings. Notice that I did not say they are "persons." They are personal beings, and they possess:

- A personal will (1 Pet. 1:12)
- Intelligent minds (2 Sam. 14:17, 20)
- Emotional responses, such as joy (Heb. 12:22; Luke 15:10) and contentiousness (Jude 9; Rev. 12:7)

Angels are incorporeal and invisible. The word *incorporeal* means "lacking in material form or substance." Angels seem to have some sort of bodies, but not the kind you can hold on to. Some of the Jewish scholars in the early church described angels as having "airy" or "fiery" bodies. For the most part, they remain invisible to our human sight.

Because their bodies are not composed of a material substance as ours are, angels do not know what it is like to get ill, to grow old, or to die.

Angels can appear as men. According to Matthew 1:20; Luke 1:11, 26–28; and John 20:12, angels can appear to humans, although normally they are invisible to us. Their resemblance can be so realistic that they are at times actually taken to be human beings. (See Hebrews 13:2.)

Angels can speak to us, in our own languages. The angel Gabriel, for example, had brief conversations first with the priest Zacharias (Luke 1:11ff) and then with Mary (Luke 1:26ff). Throughout this book, you will read contemporary accounts of people being spoken to by angels.

Angels have spatial limitations. Although they can move from place to place a lot more efficiently than we can, angels are not omnipresent. Only God is omnipresent. Angels seem to be in only one place at any one time, not everywhere; they are localized. They are also somewhat limited in when and how fast they can show up.

Daniel 9:21–23 describes Gabriel engaged in "swift flight" to travel from heaven to visit him. This implies a framework of both time and space. Gabriel didn't appear to Daniel as soon as Daniel prayed. Although the angel traveled "swiftly," it took some time to get there in response to Daniel's prayer, which indicates that the angel had a great distance to travel.

Angels are powerful but not omnipotent. "Mighty ones who do his bidding"—that's what Psalm 103:20 (NIV) calls them. We read in Matthew 28:2–7 how angels rolled the giant stone away from the front of Jesus's sepulcher. (This wheel of granite would have been five to eight feet in diameter and a foot thick, and it would have weighed several thousand pounds.)

So angels are vastly more powerful than we human beings are. Nevertheless, they have much less power than God Himself does. In fact, they are totally dependent on God for their strength, and they always exercise their strength in His service.

Angels are obedient. Angels set an example for us in the way they obediently perform God's will. In essence, they help to answer the Lord's Prayer: "Thy kingdom come. Thy will be done on earth as it is in heaven" (Matt. 6:10, KJV).

Psalm 103:20 addresses the angels directly: "Bless the LORD, you His angels, mighty in strength, who perform His word, obeying the voice of His word!"

Angels are immortal. As I mentioned above, angels don't die. Once they were created, they have never ceased to exist. Gabriel appeared to Daniel. (See Daniel 9.) Five hundred years later, this same angel named Gabriel appeared to Zacharias and then to Mary (Luke 1). Gabriel had not grown old. This wasn't Gabriel Jr. This was the same angel both times, and he is still the same today as he was over two thousand years ago when he announced the births of John the Baptist and Jesus.

Luke alludes to the immortality of angels:

> Jesus replied, "The people of this age marry and are given in marriage. But those who are considered worthy of taking part in that age and in the resurrection from the dead will neither marry nor be given in marriage, and *they can no longer die; for they are like the angels.*"
>
> —Luke 20:34–36, NIV, emphasis added

Just think about it. The same angels are still available today who held back the Red Sea for the children of Israel and who clogged up Pharaoh's chariot wheels. The same angel who is depicted in Ezekiel 9:3–6 as marking the foreheads of the people who would sigh and groan over the welfare of cities (in other words, the intercessors) is still putting marks on foreheads today (in other words, is still singling out intercessors for their service to God).

Do you think it was a once-in-a-lifetime assignment for those angels who proclaimed the Lord's birth in Bethlehem? Do you think they had to wait eons for that day to come, only to retire to heaven afterward? I don't think so. I think those same heavenly hosts are still actively announcing good news. Those angels are still on assignment, the very same ones, not a new generation of them.

Fundamentals About Angels

Before we get much farther in this book, I want to make sure that I cover all the details that we know about angels. Most of us know these things already, but it's helpful to gather everything together in one place so we don't make false assumptions about the essence of angels.

Wings. Angels may or may not have wings. In the Bible, we see some angels with two wings, some with four, and some with six. (Don't ask me how so many wings work aerodynamically!) We also see some angels with no wings at all, walking around like men or simply appearing out of nowhere.

Garments. Angels wear clothes, typically blindingly white ones. The white-robed angels who appeared at Jesus's tomb (Luke 24:4) are often called the resurrection angels, and I personally believe they are the same ones who appeared when Jesus ascended into heaven (Acts 1:10). But angelic clothing is not necessarily always white. When angels appear in the form of men, they wear whatever clothing is appropriate to the situation, as you can see throughout the Bible and in contemporary accounts.

Lightning. Sometimes, angels are too bright for people to tell what kind of garments they wear! Jesus said that He "saw Satan fall like lightning from heaven" (Luke 10:18, NKJV). Ezekiel wrote:

> As I looked, behold, a storm wind was coming from the north, a great cloud with fire flashing forth continually and a bright light around it, and in its midst something like glowing metal in the midst of the fire....They gleamed like burnished bronze....And the living beings ran to and fro like bolts of lightning.
> —Ezekiel 1:4, 7, 14

Appearance as people. Angels may look, talk, act, and dress like normal people from various cultures and ethnic origins. There are numerous reports of this. In the Bible, the accounts appear as early as the Book of Genesis, when Lot welcomed two angels with honor. But the evil men of Sodom wanted to have sexual relations with them (i.e., they really thought they were men), and they proved they were angels by the way they pulled Lot back into the safety of the house. (See Genesis 19:1–10.) The biblical passage that's most often cited with regard to angels who look like ordinary people is Hebrews 13:2: "Do not neglect to show hospitality to strangers, for by this some have entertained angels without knowing it" ("angels unawares" in the King James Version).

Angels speak. Angels speak your language. They can speak any human language or dialect that they need to speak. They also speak in a language form that is not fully known to us. (Remember the phrase "tongues of men and of angels" from 1 Corinthians 13:1.)

Sometimes angels whisper. Sometimes they speak in a normal tone of voice. Sometimes they open their mouths and shout louder than any human being could shout. They can carry on a conversation with people. Their highest joy is to broadcast the praises of God.

Angels play musical instruments. In particular, we know that they blow trumpets, which of course goes along with their role as messengers who proclaim and announce the incoming kingdom of God. (See, for example, 1 Thessalonians 4:16.) In John's apocalyptic revelation, we read, "And I saw the seven angels who stand before God, and seven trumpets were given to them.... And the seven angels who had the seven trumpets prepared themselves to sound them" (Rev. 8:2, 6).

Winds and fire. According to Hebrews 1:7, which quotes from Psalm 104:4, God "makes His angels winds, and His ministers a flame of fire." Wind and fire are often associated with the appearance of angels.

Heavenly and Earthly Realms

Sometimes it seems to me that the invisible veil that separates the heavenly (eternal) realm from the earthly (temporal) realm is becoming thinner all the time, especially when you hear testimonies like the ones I quoted in the first chapter from H. A. Baker's book *Visions Beyond the Veil.* There seems to be more visiting going back and forth between the two realms than we realize.

We know that the heavenly realm will never pass away, whereas the earthly realm will, at some point, be devoured by fire. That's why Planet Earth is called "temporal"; it's temporary. Where does this temporal world end and eternity begin? You can't tell, because so much of the kingdom of God is here now. We don't have to wait until we die to experience it. It's here already. That's what Jesus had in mind when He taught us to pray, "Thy kingdom come. Thy will be done, as in heaven, so in earth" (Luke 11:2, KJV). When we pray that prayer, we are asking God, as His children, to send reinforcements.

In heaven, they are waiting to come to our aid, and they pass over easily from the eternal to the temporal realm. We may not see them, but that doesn't mean they haven't come. (Or we *may* actually see them or sense their nearness, but that doesn't mean we're crazy!)

It's impossible to dissect and describe in minute detail how this works. One reason is because the kingdom of God is alive and active. Things keep shifting and changing. You can't stop it happening long enough to figure it all out any more than a biology student can pin down and dissect a healthy, living creature.

I remember a time when I was ministering in a Spirit-filled Episcopal church in Ohio. I looked out in the audience, and I could see a shining light over a particular person. I didn't know anything, but I was drawn to this person, and I started to talk. Then I paused and said nothing, because I didn't know what to say. From over on the side, I heard a word being spoken to me. No one else heard it. But I heard it as if it were an external, audible voice. I heard, "Her name is Anna." So I started talking again. I said, "You have an Anna anointing, like Anna in Luke 2. You're devoting your life to the Lord. In fact, your name *is* Anna!" She ended up falling out of her chair onto the floor, worshiping God.

Maybe that was the gift of the word of knowledge in operation, or it might have been a messenger angel right there giving me a little clip, sort of a cheat sheet from heaven. Somebody spoke and told me: "Her name is Anna." I sure felt like I had heavenly help.

Angels in Bennington, Vermont

Oscar Caraballo, a pastor from Puerto Rico but who lives in Vermont, has seen angels in full Technicolor. Danny Steyne of Mountain of Worship in Columbia, South Carolina, wrote up this account after the Vermont School of Prayer Conference in Burlington, Vermont, in 2006. During the evening of Wednesday, June 14, 2006, Oscar began to experience a series of events, all of which involved angels and all of which involved words about the glory of the Lord being released in Vermont and the surrounding northeastern states. After an evening full of extraordinary occurrences, the following series of events began to unfold:

> "[An] Angel came to me and said wait for further instructions from the Lord. Danny Steyne came up to me and said the Lord told him to tell me, 'You need to go!' The angel came once again and said, 'Go to Bennington, VT, now!' It was 11:00 PM by then and the drive to Bennington was 3 hours."
>
> Three hours later, Oscar arrived in Bennington. The Lord told him to go to the church building in the center of downtown Bennington, and not go home.
>
> He opened the door and began to experience a phenomenal visitation of the Lord. "I opened the door and to my surprise in the middle of the church were standing seven Angels of FIRE. To my right side was a Powerful Angel. He told me that his name is Gabriel and he introduced me to the Angels of FIRE. He told me that these were the Lord's COVENANT ANGELS. He said that power is released when they combine and work together. One of the Angels came directly towards me and he said, 'I am the one who makes things happen....' They carried the colors of the rainbow, always standing from right to left: Violet [royalty], Indigo [sovereignty], Blue [spiritual warfare], Green [growing], Yellow [mercy], Orange [worship], Red [covenant, blood of Jesus]...but they all work together....
>
> "Each of these Angels were very innocent looking, but very powerful. They were also the most loving angels I have ever encountered. They helped you fall in love with God more and more! They had so much love in them!"[8]

These angels took Oscar on a tour of Mount Snow and the mountains around New England. He saw chariots of fire and learned what would be happening in the near future. Here are two more interesting parts of his story:

> Throughout this experience, Oscar said they [the angels] were intrigued with the way we sweat. They kept saying we are made out of living water! They kept touching Oscar on the forehead when he was sweating…and they told him that they always make an effort to touch the sweat of God's children because it is so wonderful to them!!!
>
> At one point one of the angels told him that the reason they are able to be seen now is because the rain has stopped…just like a rainbow can be seen after the rain! The earth has been saturated by the rain that has been coming for years, along with the prayers. He said they told him that Mount Snow, always covered in snow, is now saturated, and that Revival would now come in the form of a "spring of living waters coming from the earth."[9]

The last line of Danny Steyne's account sounds so much like the Lord's way of doing things: "He [Oscar] asked the Lord why he would speak to him, the Lord's response was, 'Why not?'"[10]

Why not indeed! Let's be more open to hearing from God. It seems to be our often-neglected privilege to partner with the Lord and His angels. And it's good to get to know your partners a little bit, don't you think?

Father, we thank You for letting us catch glimpses of these
celestial beings we call angels. We ask You to release more
of them into our lives. Release healing angels, release
messenger angels, release warrior angels, and release the
angels who will join in with our praise and our worship.
For Jesus Christ's sake, amen.

Ye watchers and ye holy ones,
Bright seraphs, cherubim and thrones,
Raise the glad strain, Alleluia!
Cry out, dominions, princedoms, powers,
Virtues, archangels, angels' choirs,
Alleluia! Alleluia![1]

FIVE

The Characteristics of Angels

In chapter 4 we learned and reviewed certain essentials about the nature of these beings we call angels. Now I want to fine-tune our knowledge a little bit.

You can find the word *angel* or *angels* used three hundred times in the Bible. You can read one hundred four recorded angelic encounters. That's a lot, especially considering that it's only a representative sampling. The Book of Revelation records the largest number of encounters—the apostle John and others watched, listened to, or interacted with angels fifty-two times. No two of these encounters are identical.

One thing we learn from the biblical encounters is that angels are not all created equal. They were created by God to occupy certain assigned positions or "orders," if you will. Their assignments match their level of authority and status in the kingdom of God. We do well to respect this fact, even as we undoubtedly fail to comprehend or divide this reality with complete accuracy. It's not easy to define something that remains largely invisible to our earthbound eyes.

Orders of Angels

From the early medieval church, we have inherited a more or less definite idea of the orders of angels. St. Gregory the Great, who is known
as one of the doctors of the church and who died in 604, wrote about
nine orders of angels:

> We know on the authority of Scripture that there are nine orders
> of angels, viz., Angels, Archangels, Virtues, Powers, Principalities,
> Dominations, Thrones, Cherubim and Seraphim. That there are
> Angels and Archangels nearly every page of the Bible tells us, and
> the books of the Prophets talk of Cherubim and Seraphim. St. Paul,
> too, writing to the Ephesians enumerates four orders when he says:
> "above all Principality, and Power, and Virtue, and Domination";
> and again, writing to the Colossians he says: "whether Thrones, or
> Dominations, or Principalities, or Powers." If we now join these two
> lists together we have five Orders, and adding Angels and Archan-
> gels, Cherubim and Seraphim, we find nine Orders of Angels.[2]

St. Thomas Aquinas, also a doctor of the church (in the thirteenth
century), described in his treatise *Summa Theologica* three hierarchies
of angels. The ranking of each hierarchy was determined based on the
angels' proximity to God, and each of the three hierarchies contained
three orders of angels. St. Thomas included the seraphim, cherubim, and
thrones in the first hierarchy; the dominions, virtues, and powers in the
second; and the principalities, archangels, and angels in the third and
highest hierarchy.[3]

Archangels

Archangels stand (figuratively speaking) on the top rung of the corporate ladder of angels. The term *archangel* indicates that they are covering
angels who are *over* other angels.

We actually know at least two of them by name—the archangels
Gabriel and Michael. The word *archangel* was used specifically only one
time with the name of an angel following, and that's in Jude 9, with
reference to Michael: "But Michael the archangel, when he disputed with

the devil and argued about the body of Moses, did not dare pronounce against him a railing judgment, but said, 'The Lord rebuke you!'"

Various Christian traditions name other archangels, such as Raphael and Uriel—and Lucifer, the original name for satan before he fell into rebellion against God.[4]

In Scripture, instead of the name *archangel*, we more often see the phrase "anointed cherub who covers." Consider, for example, this passage about Lucifer from Ezekiel:

> You were in Eden, the garden of God; every precious stone was your covering: the ruby, the topaz and the diamond; the beryl, the onyx and the jasper; the lapis lazuli, the turquoise and the emerald; and the gold, the workmanship of your settings and sockets, was in you. On the day that you were created they were prepared.
>
> You were *the anointed cherub who covers,* and I placed you there. You were on the holy mountain of God; you walked in the midst of the stones of fire. You were blameless in your ways from the day you were created until unrighteousness was found in you.
>
> By the abundance of your trade you were internally filled with violence, and you sinned; therefore I have cast you as profane from the mountain of God. And I have destroyed you, *O covering cherub,* from the midst of the stones of fire.
>
> —Ezekiel 28:13–16, emphasis added

The term *archangel* appears in 1 Thessalonians 4:16: "For the Lord Himself will descend from heaven with a shout, with the voice of the archangel and with the trumpet of God, and the dead in Christ will rise first." And the names of Gabriel and Michael can be spotted throughout both the Old and New Testaments in accounts of angelic encounters such as Daniel's (Dan. 8–10; 12); Zacharias's (Luke 1:19); the visitation to Mary, the mother of Jesus (Luke 1:26); in accounts such as Revelation 12:7 ("And there was war in heaven, Michael and his angels waging war with the dragon. The dragon and his angels waged war…"); and the ninth verse of the Book of Jude, which I quoted just above.

Angel names

These three archangels—Michael, Gabriel, and the fallen Lucifer (and the handful of others, depending on your tradition)—are the only ones mentioned in Scripture by name. Do I believe *all* angels have names? That's a very interesting question. Some people believe that they do, although I don't know that we can be so sure. The book *The Heavens Opened* by Anna Rountree gives detailed descriptions of different angels. Almost every one of them told his name when he appeared.[5]

As for me, I've never had an angel come and give me his first name. I have, however, had angels come and make themselves known by a name that is a description of their tasks. Fairly recently, I had an angelic encounter in Knoxville, Tennessee, in which an angel announced himself as "an angel of deliverance." Is his name Deliverance? I don't know; I didn't ask! But deliverance, apparently, is his job, and I expect he's good at it. I can't count the number of times I have encountered an angel who was known as something like that.

So I do believe that angels have particular areas of stewardship. Lucifer used to be the chief minister of music in heaven. (See Ezekiel 28:13, NKJV: "The workmanship of your timbrels and pipes was prepared for you [or built into you] on the day you were created.") Because he contends actively with enemy angels, Michael is often defined as a "warrior angel." (See Revelation 12 or Daniel 12.)

Some people believe that the angel who came to stir the waters at the pool of Bethesda (John 5) was the one named Raphael, whose name means "the healing of God." People say he is sent to heal the damage done by demons. We read about Raphael (as well as Uriel, both mentioned in company with Michael and Gabriel) in the Book of Enoch, which is not included in the canon of Scripture, although it is quoted from in the Book of Jude (Jude 14).[6] Raphael is one of the principal characters in the deuterocanonical Book of Tobit, and in Jewish tradition, Uriel, whose name means "fire of God," is the cherub with the fiery sword who barred the gate to Eden.

Modern-Day Meetings With Archangels

From time to time, people report that they have received a visitation from an archangel. In the late 1970s, a man from Boise, Idaho, named Roland Buck wrote a book called *Angels on Assignment*. In this book he told story after story of true encounters with God's heavenly messengers. His own experiences included a number of encounters with the archangel Gabriel himself:

> About two o'clock one Monday morning, I was awakened when I heard noises in the downstairs part of my house. I immediately investigated to find the cause. When I did, I saw one of the most awesome sights I've ever seen. Standing in my living room were four great warrior angels, and there was tremendous activity going on in my house. Every time God has revealed himself through the visits of angels to my home or study, it has been awesome, but this seemed to be still more staggering because there was a real awareness in my spirit of the importance of what God was doing.
>
> Gabriel met me at the foot of the stairs and asked me to come into the family room. He said, "I don't want you to be frightened or fearful, but Satanic forces have started an attack against you. Just as God has his angelic organization, Satan also has his organization with princes of darkness, although he doesn't have as many, and they are not as powerful. They are not omnipresent and they cannot be everywhere at once. Their doom is already spelled out."
>
> I listened intently to Gabriel as he said he wanted to give me this assurance so that I could strengthen the bonds of God's people, and remind them of the very special time in which we are living. He said that Satan is aware of the fact that God is doing something in Boise, and he has sent princes of darkness to this area in an endeavor to hurt and rob people, to fill their minds with the things of the world and to try to hinder the work of God.
>
> He reminded me of the time when Israel was going to be delivered out of the land of Egypt, that the princes of darkness tried to stop and hinder God's work by killing all the baby boys, hoping to kill Moses. He did the same thing after Jesus was born.

I thought it was extremely interesting when Gabriel said that Satan does not know what is going to happen. He cannot foretell the future and he cannot read the minds of people. He is extremely nervous because he doesn't know exactly what is going on, but he is hoping somehow to slow down whatever it is that God is doing! Gabriel said since the Holy Spirit monitors everything on earth, he will not allow him to do this. When he sees the activity of Satan becoming dangerous, he dispatches hosts of angels to straighten out the situation.

My attention was drawn to a special angel there, who was very huge and warlike! As I looked at him, I noticed that in spite of this fierceness, there was also a tremendous resemblance to Gabriel! I will never forget the eyes of this large angel because they looked like pools of fire! I was observing his strength and might when Gabriel very simply told me that God had sent his mightiest warring angel to clear away and push back those princes of darkness. I could hardly breathe, it was so awe-inspiring, because this was my introduction to MICHAEL!

It is virtually impossible to describe the radiation and the glow that came from their presence. I could sense compassion and love, and the fruit of the Holy Spirit, because the atmosphere of heaven is the nature of Jesus. All of these angelic beings have that same nature and tremendous compassion....

Gabriel informed me that a battle was going on that night and these warring angels in the living room were actually directing the armies of heaven who were pushing back the forces of darkness. Michael and the three captains who were there with him were receiving messages from the Holy Spirit, as he monitored all of the activities, and in turn they were giving messages in languages I didn't understand, to angel leaders who were carrying out the battle.

Michael said that until the appointed time when Satan would be cast out completely, God allows this, and there is a constant dispersing and scattering of evil forces by the warring angels. He told me there was nothing to fear because the angels were overcoming the enemy, guarding and protecting us! Hallelujah!...

Michael said, "Up until the appointed time, our task is not to destroy Satan, but to scatter the forces of darkness, to hold them in abeyance, to overcome them and to keep them from God's people."[7]

Cherubim and Seraphim

Ezekiel's visions of God's throne are the greatest and most mysterious—even disturbing—visions in the Bible. Ezekiel describes the cherubim:

> Now the cherubim were standing on the right side of the temple when the man entered, and the cloud filled the inner court. Then the glory of the LORD went up from the cherub to the threshold of the temple, and the temple was filled with the cloud and the court was filled with the brightness of the glory of the LORD. Moreover, the sound of the wings of the cherubim was heard as far as the outer court, like the voice of God Almighty when He speaks....
>
> The cherubim appeared to have the form of a man's hand under their wings. Then I looked, and behold, four wheels beside the cherubim, one wheel beside each cherub; and the appearance of the wheels was like the gleam of a Tarshish stone. As for their appearance, all four of them had the same likeness, as if one wheel were within another wheel. When they moved, they went in any of their four directions without turning as they went; but they followed in the direction which they faced, without turning as they went.
>
> Their whole body, their backs, their hands, their wings and the wheels were full of eyes all around, the wheels belonging to all four of them. The wheels were called in my hearing, the whirling wheels.
>
> And each one had four faces. The first face was the face of a cherub, the second face was the face of a man, the third the face of a lion, and the fourth the face of an eagle.
>
> —Ezekiel 10:3–5, 8–14

The Hebrew used in this chapter is very obscure, mixing masculine and feminine forms, singular and plural. Perhaps Ezekiel was trying to describe the unity and the plurality of the divine presence.

Earlier in the book he describes the cherubim as living creatures who are "fiery." They are humanoids with four hands, four wings, and four faces. One face is human, the face on the left looks like a bull's face, the face on the right looks like a lion's face, and the last face looks like the face of an eagle. "And each went straight forward; wherever the spirit was about to go, they would go, without turning as they went" (Ezek. 1:12).

How could Ezekiel describe something that is beyond words? He (and others, such as John as he was writing the Book of Revelation) did the best he could do to describe something that you would have to see yourself to believe.

Moses was instructed to portray cherubim on the ark of the covenant. The specific description is found in Exodus 25:18–22 (and is alluded to in Hebrews 9:5). The singular of cherubim is "cherub"; there were two separate ones on opposite ends of the ark, made of one piece with the mercy seat.

The Bible tells us that God "rides upon a cherub." I'd like to see that sometime! Look at Psalm 18:10, "He rode upon a cherub and flew; and He sped upon the wings of the wind," and 2 Samuel 22:11, "And He rode on a cherub and flew; and He appeared on the wings of the wind." I guess it's only naturally supernatural for Him to do so. After all, He is "enthroned above the cherubim" (2 Sam. 6:2).

Seraphim

Like *cherubim*, the word *seraphim* is plural; the singular form is "seraph." The word means "burning one." The seraphim are described as having six wings, and they lift up a continual cry of, "Holy, Holy, Holy, is the Lord of hosts, the whole earth is full of His glory" (Isa. 6:3).

Isaiah saw them "in the year of King Uzziah's death," and his life was never the same again:

> I saw the Lord sitting on a throne, lofty and exalted, with the train
> of His robe filling the temple. Seraphim stood above Him, each

having six wings: with two he covered his face, and with two he covered his feet, and with two he flew....

Then I said, "Woe is me, for I am ruined! Because I am a man of unclean lips, and I live among a people of unclean lips; for my eyes have seen the King, the LORD of hosts."

Then one of the seraphim flew to me with a burning coal in his hand, which he had taken from the altar with tongs. He touched my mouth with it and said, "Behold, this has touched your lips; and your iniquity is taken away and your sin is forgiven."

—Isaiah 6:1–2, 5–7

Do you see the connection? The seraphim cry "holy, holy, holy" to each other all the time—and they bring purity to sinful human beings so that we can approach the throne of God. I think that when we experience the manifest presence of God and feel utterly undone and small, the seraphim have been released to come into our realm.

The seraphim aren't as hard to describe as the cherubim, but just the same, they're far outside our normal experience. Christians over the centuries have pictured their six-winged bodies differently. Daniel and Ezekiel recorded only very brief accounts, while Isaiah and John attempted to describe them in more detail. Some artists have pictured only two seraphim, one on either side of the Lord enthroned. Others have felt that there were four of them, like the four winds or four corners of the earth, and they depicted them at the four supporting corners of magnificent churches, supporting the dome of heaven. Some artists have depicted the six-winged seraphim as a cluster of wings. But some early Christians thought the wings were covering the Lord on His throne.

I need to remind you angels are incorporeal—they are spirits; they have no bodies. And yet they are described as if they do. In very important ways, our halting effort to describe such spectacular creatures does at least manage to capture certain truths about them. They are bright and fiery, purifying everything they touch. They have angelic voices, eyes, wings, hands, and feet with which to praise and serve God

Almighty. Maybe someday you and I will be privileged to see them in action!

Other Categories of Angels

Besides the archangels, the cherubim, and the seraphim, Scripture leads us to believe that there are several other possible categories of angels. I want to focus on five of them.

1. The angel of the Lord
2. Guardian angels
3. Angels assigned to churches
4. Angels of great authority
5. Strong angels

The angel of the Lord

Throughout Scripture we find occasional references to "the angel of the Lord" and "the angel of His presence." What does this mean?

> In all their affliction He was afflicted, and *the angel of His presence* saved them; in His love and in His mercy He redeemed them, and He lifted them and carried them all the days of old.
> —Isaiah 63:9, emphasis added

> Behold, I am going to send an angel before you to guard you along the way and to bring you into the place which I have prepared. Be on your guard before him and obey his voice; do not be rebellious toward him, for he will not pardon your transgression, since *My name is in him.*
> —Exodus 23:20–21, emphasis added

> He said, "My presence shall go with you, and I will give you rest." Then he [Moses] said to Him, "If Your presence does not go with us, do not lead us up from here."
> —Exodus 33:14–15

Supernatural presences were thought to dwell within a name. Hence, an "angel of His presence" carries God's manifest presence into a place.

This is akin to "the angel of the Lord." For example, consider the familiar words of Psalm 34:7: "The angel of the LORD encamps around those who fear Him, and rescues them." Also recall 1 Chronicles 21:16: "Then David lifted up his eyes and saw the angel of the LORD standing between earth and heaven, with his drawn sword in his hand stretched out over Jerusalem. Then David and the elders, covered with sackcloth, fell on their faces."

Sometimes an appearance of the angel of the Lord can be termed a *theophany,* a visible manifestation of the Lord Jesus Christ before His incarnation as a human being. The story of the fiery furnace in Daniel 3 is often cited as an example. Who was the fourth man who appeared with the three Hebrew men in the midst of the flames, who came to preserve their lives, comfort them, and demonstrate the sovereign power of God? It could have been another kind of angel, but more likely it was a preincarnate appearance of the Lord Jesus Christ. Who were the three strangers who visited Abram when he was encamped at Mamre? (See Genesis 18.) Was this Jesus in preincarnate form, accompanied by two angels?

Surely many such angelic encounters have gone unrecorded, nor are they confined to the Old Testament. Up to the present day, the angel of the Lord comes to bring *Him* into a situation. When angels of His presence show up, they usher in what we call the manifest presence of God. What they bring is "thicker," very powerful. Some element of God Himself shows up. In comes a wave of glory, as if an angel has parted the veil. *Swoosh!* In comes a breath of the heavenly atmosphere.

Guardian angels

Some people just assume that everyone has a personal guardian angel, while others think that's only a quaint folk belief, especially since Scripture only notes the existence of such angels in two passages, both of which reflect Jewish beliefs of the time:

And He called a child to Himself and set him before them, and said, "Truly I say to you, unless you are converted and become like children, you will not enter the kingdom of heaven....See that you do not despise one of these little ones, for I say to you that their angels in heaven continually see the face of My Father who is in heaven."

—Matthew 18:2–3, 10

When he knocked at the door of the gate, a servant-girl named Rhoda came to answer. When she recognized Peter's voice, because of her joy she did not open the gate, but ran in and announced that Peter was standing in front of the gate. They said to her, "You are out of your mind!" But she kept insisting that it was so. They kept saying, "It is his angel."

—Acts 12:13–15

Experientially, I think many of us can testify to angelic protection, either on our own behalf or on the behalf of a family member or friend. I know I can.

Angels assigned to churches

In a similar way, it is likely that churches have angels assigned to them. We think of the phrase "to the angel of..." before the names of each of the seven churches in the Book of Revelation, chapters 2 and 3. Each of the seven utterances begins in the same way: "And to the angel of the church [in/of]..." Ephesus, Smyrna, Pergamum, Thyatira, Sardis, Philadelphia, and Laodicea... "write..." Specific, pointed messages of both encouragement and rebuke are given. What would the angels of these churches do with these words? Why would John be like a messenger to the angels of these churches? Were these words addressed to actual angels, to human overseers of the churches, or to the prevailing spirit of each church—or to a combination of these possibilities? This is another case where we have more questions than answers.

The previous chapter, however, does state quite simply, "The seven stars [that John saw] are the angels of the seven churches" (Rev. 1:20).

The Greek word *angelos* is used, from which our English word *angel* derives, and that means "messenger or courier." These particular angels are *of* the seven churches.

Angels of great authority

Angels (copied by their evil counterparts) seem to have territorial assignments. These are angels of great authority. Later in the Book of Revelation, we read, "After these things I saw another angel coming down from heaven, having great authority, and the earth was illumined with his glory. And he cried out with a mighty voice, saying, 'Fallen, fallen is Babylon the great!'" (Rev. 18:1–2).

Such angels of great authority perhaps rule over spheres of authority on the earth, such as cities and regions. Clement of Alexandria, an early Greek theologian, seems to have believed this was true. Referring to Daniel 10:13–21, he wrote, "The presiding powers of the angels have been distributed according to the nations and the cities."[8]

Strong angels

It may or may not be helpful to differentiate angels of great authority from "strong angels," which is another phrase used in the Book of Revelation.

> And I saw a strong angel proclaiming with a loud voice, "Who is worthy to open the book and to break its seals?"
>
> —Revelation 5:2

> I saw another strong angel coming down out of heaven, clothed with a cloud; and the rainbow was upon his head, and his face was like the sun, and his feet like pillars of fire; and he had in his hand a little book which was open. He placed his right foot on the sea and his left on the land; and he cried out with a loud voice, as when a lion roars; and when he had cried out, the seven peals of thunder uttered their voices.
>
> —Revelation 10:1–3

> Then a strong angel took up a stone like a great millstone and threw it into the sea, saying, "So will Babylon, the great city, be thrown down with violence, and will not be found any longer."
>
> —Revelation 18:21

Strong angels are *strong*! Their words carry great authority as they make declarations about heavenly decisions and major shifts.

We could say more along these lines about different types of angels, but I'll reserve that discussion for the next chapter, in which I describe the incredible variety of angelic assignments.

The Company of Heaven

The range and extent of the angelic realm blows your mind, doesn't it? In spite of our earnest efforts to understand God's kingdom, we end up with only a partial idea of the infinite variety and unreserved power of these fellow servants of ours.

Here we have a host of superbly fashioned beings who serve Him (and, by extension, us) with an amazing combination of complete submission to a defined military ranking and complete, joyful liberty. The angels love the way God created them so much that they probably don't evaluate it—because their attention is so much on God Himself. They're eager for His next word to them, eager for their next assignment in the service of the Most Holy One.

With His help, and theirs, we can obtain a degree of the same single-hearted focus. That's my goal, until the day when I graduate to join the heavenly chorus in limitless praise and worship.

Father, we call on You to release Your angels right now to places of darkness, where Your fiery ones can shed Your light. May Your kingdom come and Your will be done everywhere on Earth as it is in heaven. We see that this world is not a safe place, and we trust that You will send angelic guards to protect us and guide us. May the angels of Your presence be released in our midst. You are the same yesterday, today, and forever. Amen!

God, that madest earth and Heaven, darkness and light,
Who the day for toil hast given, for rest the night,
May Thine angel guards defend us,
Slumber sweet Thy mercy send us;
Holy dreams and hopes attend us, all through the night.[1]

S I X

Angelic Assignments

As I mentioned in the previous chapter, angels definitely seem to have particular areas of stewardship. In essence, they have *assignments*. Their assignments fit within the context of their three primary functions. Here's a quick review for you:

1. Angels give service to God—worshiping God eternally. (See Psalm 148:2.)
2. Angels give service to people, especially believers. (See Hebrews 1:7, 14.)
3. Angels perform God's word. (See Psalm 103:20–21.)

Their assignment to worship God is their highest and grandest one, but it is far from being merely the "standard-issue" angelic assignment (and therefore the most mundane one). Angels define worship. They worshiped at Creation. They certainly worshiped at the birth of Jesus the Messiah, showing up in the sky over the shepherd's field. They still worship now that the church lives under the new covenant; they will worship Him until the Second Coming of Jesus and beyond, to all eternity.

Nobody needs to pray that the angels will keep worshiping. It keeps happening without human cooperation. Our privilege is to participate to some degree in it, especially after we go to be with the Lord forever. The twenty-four elders cast down their crowns before Him, and the angels of God join with the people of God to declare, eternally, that He is worthy.

But while we're still here in this world, we do pray about a lot of other matters, and God assigns angels to perform His will. We don't pray only the sweeping prayers such as, "Thy kingdom come. Thy will be done on earth as it is in heaven." We also pray, "Give us this day our daily bread" and "Lead us not into temptation." We pray very specific prayers, such as, "Lord, please heal this," "Father, help me forgive so-and-so," and "Holy Spirit, provide protection for my family on our trip."

Our prayers are often prayed in direct response to divine nudges. We don't just dream them up all by ourselves. Therefore, when we pray, we are releasing an invitation or request back to God. In essence, our best prayers originate with Him. And in response to our requests, He often assigns an angel or two to meet our need. This is the way it has worked since the beginning of time. Angels have always been waiting and ready to act according to God's command in response to human prayers. They were with the prophets of old, and they visited priests of the old covenant. They helped Daniel in the lions' den. They released spectacular judgments on the Lord's behalf. They strengthened Jesus in the Garden of Gethsemane.

Other times, He plants a word in our spirits, and we give voice to it in a declarative manner. We might call that a *rhema* word or a gift of faith. We may actually say something like, "I call forth you angels to come and do this!" But it's not as if we originated the concept—God Himself did. Angels aren't at our beck and call; they are at His, and so are we. Therefore, a man or a woman who is in a relationship with God can sometimes tap into the heartbeat of heaven and give voice to God's divine will for that moment in time.

Coming full circle, I don't want to leave the impression that all angelic assignments require human involvement, because they don't. A long time ago, God assigned His angels to perform certain functions above and beyond worshiping Him. We assume that many of them have stayed with their first assignments, with no human involvement whatsoever. For instance, He assigned "cherubim and the flaming sword" to guard the gates of Eden (Gen. 3:24).

Angels do seem to "specialize" in particular duties. However, there is no rigid dividing line between different types of assignments. For example, when an angel brings someone a message, the word can provide guidance, protection, or deliverance—or all three. As you will see in this chapter, we can say quite a bit about what God assigns angels to do, but our explanations come from the limited perspective of our little patch of Planet Earth, which is our "observation deck." For the most part, we can only stand in awe. God's angelic host is magnificent, and the Lord God is the most magnificent of all!

Ushering in God's Presence

Have you ever been in a worship gathering where you could tell that the spiritual "temperature" went up a notch? Something seemed extra special about it. You may have identified it as what I call the "manifest presence of God."

In the natural, this happens all the time—not the manifest presence of God, but rather some natural "presence" riding into a room with a person. Even when your co-worker comes back from a vacation, he or she can bring a sense of relaxation along. Or the opposite can occur: your spouse can come home from work bringing along all the tension of the difficult day. I believe that the angels, who spend so much of their time before the throne of God, can't help but bring His presence to a place! Sometimes that presence is a perceptible aroma or a feeling of electricity or a visible light. Other times it's an awe-inspiring, even weighty feeling of pressure. God's holiness supercharges the atmosphere, and that affects His angels, who can't help but bring an extra wave of His holiness wherever they go.

I remember being in Kansas City in 1975 at the National Men's Shepherds Conference, which was held in the Municipal Auditorium. A lot of the "generals of the faith" were there, most of whom have now gone on to be with the Lord. I remember Ern Baxter delivering one of the greatest messages I've ever heard, called "Thy Kingdom Come." He had an unusual degree of authority on him, and he was declaring the government of God. Something holy happened in worship, prophetic words were released, and a shift occurred. It wasn't just the generals of faith who were present—some generals of heaven showed up, too. In response to the holy presence of God, every single man took off his shoes in a unified response of humility. We just got on our faces. It was the least we could do. None of us had crowns on our heads that we could cast before God, but we had shoes on our feet. It was a true *kairos* moment, where heaven and Earth met, a holy crossroads. Angels were present, probably by the thousands, and we recognized that we were standing on holy ground. The climate shifted enormously, from one of familiarity with God to one of the fear of the Lord. Angels came to the Municipal Auditorium, carrying the golden light of heaven to the earth.

We can assume that, whenever we feel God's presence, angels are in a place, regardless of whether or not we can see them. Our response is always going to be worship—holy, holy, holy is the Lord of hosts!

Angelic Direction

Besides conveying God's presence when they come, angels have specific jobs to do when they arrive.

I believe that the tasks God has assigned to angels fall into two major categories: *direction* and *protection*. Obviously, these categories overlap and mingle, just as they do with our natural human tasks When you drive your children someplace in the car, you are providing them with direction (by steering the car to a destination) and protection (by keeping them safe from traffic, weather, and other potential hazards). But let's go ahead and take a look at each category, so we can better appreciate what angels do.

First, what are some of the ways that angels bring God's *direction* to us? Here are four of them:

1. Angels deliver God's messages.
2. Angels release dreams, revelation, and understanding.
3. Angels give guidance.
4. Angels impart strength.

In one way or another, all of these functions provide direction.

Angels delivering God's messages

What would we do without the services of God's angelic messengers? If you sit down and start turning the pages of your Bible, you will find story after story about angels bringing messages from God. They announce forthcoming events. They pronounce God's judgments. They bring encouragement. They "direct traffic," telling people what to do, how to do it, and when to do it. Here's a quick sampling of such angelic "instant messaging," from both the Old and New Testaments:

- **Joshua 5:13–15.** Joshua encountered a commanding angel who tells him how to take Jericho: "Now it came about when Joshua was by Jericho, that he lifted up his eyes and looked, and behold, a man was standing opposite him with his sword drawn in his hand, and Joshua went to him and said to him, 'Are you for us or for our adversaries?' He said, 'No; rather I indeed come now as captain of the host of the Lord.' And Joshua fell on his face to the earth, and bowed down, and said to him, 'What has my lord to say to his servant?' The captain of the Lord's host said to Joshua, 'Remove your sandals from your feet, for the place where you are standing is holy.' And Joshua did so."

- **Judges 13:3–21.** The angel of the Lord visited Manoah and his barren wife, telling them that she would bear a son and instructing them specifically about what to do: "Now see to it that you drink no wine or other fermented drink and that you do not eat anything unclean, because you will conceive and give birth to a son. No razor may be used on his head, because the boy is to be a Nazirite, set apart to God from birth, and he will begin the deliverance of Israel from the hands of the Philistines" (vv. 4–5, NIV). The promised baby boy was Samson.

- **Luke 1:19–20.** An archangel brought a message to Zacharias: "The angel answered and said to him, 'I am Gabriel, who stands in the presence of God, and I have been sent to speak to you and to bring you this good news. And behold, you shall be silent and unable to speak until the day when these things take place, because you did not believe my words, which will be fulfilled in their proper time.'"

- **Luke 1:28–37.** Gabriel brought a message to Mary: "And coming in, he said to her, 'Greetings, favored one! The Lord is with you....Do not be afraid, Mary; for you have found favor with God. And behold, you will conceive in your womb and bear a son, and you shall name Him Jesus. He will be great and will be called the Son of the Most High; and the Lord God will give Him the throne of His father David; and He will reign over the house of Jacob forever, and His kingdom will have no end....The Holy Spirit will come upon you, and the power of the Most High will overshadow you; and for that reason the holy Child shall be called the Son of God. And behold, even your relative Elizabeth has also conceived a son in her old age; and she who was called barren is now in her sixth month. For nothing will be impossible with God.'"

- **Luke 2:10.** Angels filled the sky, and a spokesman-angel announced Jesus's birth to the shepherds: "Do not be afraid; for behold, I bring you good news of great joy which will be for all the people."

- **Matthew 1:20; 2:13, 19–20.** Angelic messengers spoke to Joseph in dreams to direct him to take Mary as his wife, to take Mary and the baby Jesus to Egypt for safety before Herod had all of the infants murdered, and to bring them back to Nazareth after Herod's death.

- **Matthew 28:1–7.** An angel proclaimed the resurrection of Jesus: "He is not here, for He has risen, just as He said. Come, see the place where He was lying. Go quickly and tell His disciples that He has risen from the dead; and behold, He is going ahead of you into Galilee, there you will see Him; behold, I have told you" (vv. 6–7).

Angels releasing dreams, revelation, and understanding

An angel in a dream told Joseph how to take care of Mary and Jesus. Other times, angels release revelational understanding without speaking in dreams. Here is a contemporary example, told by a man named Terry Law, in which the pastor named Roland Buck (who was mentioned in the previous chapter of this book) obtained a detailed understanding of Law's past and future by means of angelic revelation:

As a thirteen-year-old boy, I attended a camp meeting at Nanoose Bay in Vancouver Island, British Columbia. One night a speaker from the American Assemblies of God gave a stirring call for commitment and a challenge for missions, and the Holy Spirit began to move on me....

...[I stayed after] everyone else left for the night, and the lights were turned out. Midnight passed, 1:00 a.m. passed, and then around 2:00 a.m., the evangelist returned.

His name was Dwight McLaughlin, and he had left his Bible on the pulpit. I was sitting on a bench in the shadows where he could not see me, but I could see him in the moonlight. I sat motionless, but he sensed someone was there and called out. When I answered, he felt his way to where I sat in a back corner.

He said, "You know, the Lord must have sent me to you," and explained that he had awakened and felt impressed to go get his Bible. Then he asked if he could pray for me. When he laid his hand on me, warmth radiated through me. I started to tremble.

He said, "Young man, I see a vision. God has called you, and He is going to send you around the world to preach the gospel. I see crowds of thousands and hundreds of thousands."...

Years later, in 1977, I was traveling with my music group Living Sound and came to minister at Roland Buck's church in Boise, Idaho. Roland and I were outside the church one night sitting in his car when he told me a story.

He began by saying very quietly, "Terry, I talked with Gabriel last week."

At the time, I knew no more about angels than the average Christian, perhaps less than some, and I said, "Gabriel who?"...

[Two years later, I returned to his church.] As my co-evangelist, Gordon Calmeyer, and I were sitting at breakfast with Roland one morning, Gordon shocked me with a question for Roland about angels.

"Well, pastor," he said, "if these angels are talking to you all the time, and your church is a strong supporter of our ministry, why don't you ask the angels about us?"...

...Roland sat there with a slight smile and did not say anything. We went our separate ways, and I forgot about the conversation.

Three months later I was asked to appear on a national Christian television program to introduce Roland....Before the program went on the air, we were in a room backstage together, just the two of us.

He said, "Terry do you remember when you were a thirteen-year-old and attended a camp meeting in Canada?"

I had never told another soul what happened that night.

Roland said, "Do you remember about 2:00 a.m., the camp evangelist"—and he actually named Dwight McLaughlin—"walked into the building? Do you remember that you were sitting there praying, and he walked over and laid hands on you?"

I said, "Roland, how do you know about that night?"

He looked at me and just smiled. I exclaimed, "Are you kidding me? The angels told you this?"

He nodded and said the angels had awakened McLaughlin because that was the night God had chosen for my ordination into ministry.

"The angels told me a lot about you," he said. "They told me of times in your childhood when you went through great difficulties. You had to learn as a child to stand up against odds and overcome them. God was getting you ready for your ministry. He was building iron into your character."[2]

Stories like this one make me wonder—how much of what we call prophetic revelation is actually handed to us by our fellow servants, the angels? The entire Book of the Revelation of Jesus Christ was communicated to John by His angel. Daniel had such profoundly disturbing experiences that only an angel could interpret them for him. (See Daniel 8:15–26; 9:20–27.) Quite likely, angels are helping you understand about angels as you read this book!

On October 4, 2004, I was in Colorado Springs, and I had a dream encounter that was about receiving interpretation. In the dream, I was with John Paul Jackson. (One seer was with another seer.) John Paul turned to me and said, "How do you do that?"

I smiled, saying, "I have help!" Then I turned and said, "He hands me scrolls, and I read them." When I turned, there was an angel by my side handing me a scroll to read.

For a short time after that dream, maybe three or four days, I had sort of a holy buzz that was all around my head, some kind of supernatural capacity to understand and interpret revelation. I didn't let a lot of people know about this, but I could tell what God was speaking to people, and I could interpret it supernaturally. I have to believe that the scroll-bearing angel stepped out of my dream and into my waking life.

Angels giving God's guidance

Besides releasing dreams, revelation, and understanding, angels give direct guidance. That's what happened to Philip before he met up with the Ethiopian eunuch: "An angel of the Lord spoke to Philip saying, 'Get up and go south to the road that descends from Jerusalem to Gaza'" (Acts 8:26). It was as if the angel handed him a set of directions.

That's also what happened when Abraham's servant went off in search of the right bride for Isaac. (See Genesis 24:7, 40.) An angel "went before him" so that he would find the way to the right place at the right time when the right girl was right there.

Paul, when he was on board the storm-tossed ship, had an angel come to give him guidance for the crew and other passengers: "This very night an angel of the God to whom I belong and whom I serve stood before me, saying, 'Do not be afraid, Paul; you must stand before Caesar; and behold, God has granted you all those who are sailing with you.' Therefore, keep up your courage, men, for I believe God that it will turn out exactly as I have been told. But we must run aground on a certain island" (Acts 27:23–26).

Jumping back to the Old Testament, we see an angel confronting Balaam, literally directing traffic by redirecting his donkey—who opened his mouth and *spoke* to his master before the angel did:

> Then the Lord opened the eyes of Balaam, and he saw the angel of the Lord standing in the way with his drawn sword in his hand; and he bowed all the way to the ground. The angel of the Lord said to him, "Why have you struck your donkey these three times? Behold, I have come out as an adversary, because your way was contrary to me. But the donkey saw me and turned aside from me these three times. If she had not turned aside from me, I would surely have killed you just now, and let her live."
>
> Balaam said to the angel of the Lord, "I have sinned, for I did not know that you were standing in the way against me. Now then, if it is displeasing to you, I will turn back."
>
> But the angel of the Lord said to Balaam, "Go with the men,

but you shall speak only the word which I tell you." So Balaam went along with the leaders of Balak.

—Numbers 22:31–35

Talk about direct angelic guidance! It looks like it can get a little dangerous sometimes.

Angels imparting strength

Sometimes angels come to impart encouragement and strength more than anything else.

In Genesis 16, we read about Sarai's Egyptian maid Hagar, who was forced to become pregnant and then as a result was abused by Sarai, to the point that she ran away into the wilderness in distress. God sent an angel to comfort her:

But the Angel of the Lord found her by a spring of water in the wilderness on the road to Shur. And He said, Hagar, Sarai's maid, where did you come from, and where are you intending to go? And she said, I am running away from my mistress Sarai.

The Angel of the Lord said to her, Go back to your mistress and [humbly] submit to her control. Also the Angel of the Lord said to her, I will multiply your descendants exceedingly, so that they shall not be numbered for multitude. And the Angel of the Lord continued, See now, you are with child and shall bear a son, and shall call his name Ishmael [God hears], because the Lord has heard and paid attention to your affliction. And he [Ishmael] will be as a wild ass among men; his hand will be against every man and every man's hand against him, and he will live to the east and on the borders of all his kinsmen.

So she called the name of the Lord Who spoke to her, You are a God of seeing, for she said, Have I [not] even here [in the wilderness] looked upon Him Who sees me [and lived]? Or have I here also seen [the future purposes or designs of] Him Who sees me? Therefore the well was called Beer-lahai-roi [A well to the Living One Who sees me]; it is between Kadesh and Bered.

—Genesis 16:7–14, AMP

Angels came to strengthen Jesus after His forty-day fast in the wilderness. (See Matthew 4:11; Mark 1:13.) Again, an angel came to His aid when He agonized in Gethsemane before He was crucified (Luke 22:43).

During a time of distress, angels were used to impart God's strength to Daniel (Dan. 10:18). As he and many others have discovered, one touch from an angel is enough to send a power surge through our mortal bodies.

After Elijah defeated the prophets of Baal, he ran into the wilderness, afraid and exhausted. There, an angel strengthened him not only with words but also with supernatural food: "He lay down and slept under a juniper tree; and behold, there was an angel touching him, and he said to him, 'Arise, eat.' Then he looked and behold, there was at his head a bread cake baked on hot stones, and a jar of water. So he ate and drank and lay down again. The angel of the LORD came again a second time and touched him and said, 'Arise, eat, because the journey is too great for you.' So he arose and ate and drank, and went in the strength of that food forty days and forty nights to Horeb, the mountain of God" (1 Kings 19:5–8).

Thank You, Lord, for sending Your angels to bring us divine strength and encouragement.

Angelic Protection

Next, we turn to the angelic assignments that can be loosely categorized as angelic *protection*. When angels come to protect the people to whom God sends them, sometimes they bring *deliverance* in their wings. Other times they bring some type of *healing*. And at the end of a saint's life on Earth, they provide a protective *escort* to heaven. These are all aspects of protection.

Angels protect isolated individuals, and they protect groups of people, families, and churches from harm. They protect soldiers on battlefields from injury; they protect the poor and disenfranchised from mistreatment and hunger; they stand watch night and day over households where people have called upon the blood of Jesus. We know about angelic protection from both Scripture and our personal experiences.

Angels providing protection

In chapter 5, I mentioned "guardian angels." Matthew 18:10 is the verse from which we obtain our understanding of guardian angels for children. I see no reason why angels would not also be assigned to guard and protect adults as well. After all, grown-ups are His children, too.

Psalm 91:11–12 reads, "For He will give His angels charge concerning you, to guard you in all your ways. They will bear you up in their hands, that you do not strike your foot against a stone."

Most of us have heard about many examples of angelic protection. A family working with Wycliffe Bible Translators in Bolivia gives an especially clear illustration below. I have condensed an account that was written by the missionary mom. Her two sons, Doug and Dennis, who were seven and nine years old, were playing, and they had dug a shallow cave in a hillside of dried mud. Suddenly, it shifted and collapsed, trapping both boys. Their friend, Mark, ran for help.

> Inside the cave, Doug had been slapped down on his chest. His face was smashed into the dirt, but a pocket of air helped him breathe.
>
> "Dennis, can you hear me?"
>
> His voice seemed to make no sound at all, but he felt a slight movement beneath him. "Dennis," Doug went on. "I can't move. I can't breathe!"
>
> He felt another wiggle. An ant crawled onto his face, then another. The first sting came. It was on his eyelid.
>
> "Dennis, I can't talk...the air's going away."
>
> The ants were all over him now, stinging. "Dennis, I think we're maybe going to die." He began to struggle. Dirt filled his mouth.
>
> And then Douglas stopped talking. He even stopped struggling for air. For there, next to him, was an angel. He stood bright, strong.

"Dennis!" Doug called softly, his voice relaxed. "Dennis, there's an *angel* here. I can see him plain as anything. He's bright. He's trying to help us." Doug felt one oh-so-slight movement.

"He's not doing anything. But Dennis...if we die now...it's not so bad...." Doug lost consciousness.[3]

Mark reached the house, screaming for help. Men came with picks and shovels. Mark showed them where to dig.

Seconds later one of the shovels touched softness. Seconds again and Doug's back and legs were free. Strong arms pulled him from the earth. Dennis' form appeared beneath him.

Neither boy was breathing. Their skin was blue. They lay on the red earth, their bodies so terribly small....

Then Douglas moved. A moment later Dennis stirred....

"Mommy!" Douglas said as soon as he opened his eyes. "Do you know what I saw? An angel!"

"Shh, sweetheart. Don't try to talk yet."

[The next day, the doctor told us that] another two minutes...and the lack of oxygen would have damaged the boys' brains. But because they had not spent themselves struggling, the doctor said, they had just exactly enough oxygen to come through the experience without damage. And the reason they had not struggled, all of us knew, was the angel—the angel who kept them from being afraid.[4]

In his book *Angels Around Us*, Douglas Connelly tells the story of a woman from his church:

A woman was in the critical care unit with a raging infection. She was not expected to survive. I was her pastor at the time, and as I stood by her bedside and talked to her, she would respond only with nods or whispers. Finally she said, "Who is the man standing in the corner, dressed in white? He's been standing there all night and all day today."

When I looked at the corner of the room, no one was there. I said, "What does he look like?"

"Can't you see him?" she replied. "He's all in white, and he is so strong. It's like he is standing guard. I'm almost afraid to speak in his presence."

I asked the nurse when I left the room if the patient had said anything about a man in her room. The nurse reassured me that the woman was just hallucinating. "Has she seen anything else that wasn't there?" I asked.

"Oh, no, she is very perceptive—except for the man in white!" As I walked out of the hospital I was convinced that what this dear child of God saw in her room was not a hallucination. It was a very real angel of God.[5]

This "man in white" had indeed come to guard her—or perhaps to wait until it was time to take her home to the Father. We'll look at that angelic assignment next.

Angels escorting saints to heaven

Many people have had experiences confirming that angels arrive when a saint of God dies, specifically to escort that person's soul to the heavenly realm where he or she will dwell forever. Surely we can't get there on our own, so this must be true. What a comforting fact.

Not long ago, I was told of an event when a believing mother went home to be with the Lord. Her three daughters reported that she had an angelic encounter. Evidently, an angel came into her bedroom and the mother was caught up. They thought at first that maybe she was out of her mind, because she started talking about the things she was seeing. Her husband had passed on just a few months before, and she said she was looking for him. Then she saw someone else she knew, someone who had died already. Then, with the angel directing her on this side of death, she saw Jesus. She started declaring, "It's Jesus! I see Jesus. I see Jesus." At that, of course, her daughters realized that she was on the edge of death, so they agreed to bless their mother, and she was gone a little later. Perhaps the angel came to carry her home.

We regularly quote a couple of psalms that refer to the time of death. Psalm 116:15 reads, "Precious in the sight of the LORD is the death of his saints" (KJV). Psalm 23:4 is even more familiar to us: "Even though I walk through the valley of the shadow of death, I fear no evil, for You are with me; Your rod and Your staff, they comfort me."

But the best biblical confirmation of the idea of angels carrying people home to God comes from the story about a beggar named Lazarus. Luke 16:22 literally reads, "Now the poor man died and was carried away by the angels to Abraham's bosom," which means he was taken to paradise or heaven. Angels took him there.

We don't know how it goes at the death of someone who doesn't belong to God. When the rich man in the story dies, no angels are mentioned. I don't know about you, but I know I'd much rather be assigned an angelic escort when I'm about to draw my final breath.

Angels are involved at the beginnings and the endings of our lives, with everything in between—and beyond!

Angels bringing deliverance

Often, angels deliver us from harm. Psalm 34:7 says, "The angel of the LORD encamps around those who fear Him, and rescues them." The angel of the Lord not only stands watch ("encamps"), but he also reaches out to rescue those who are sinking.

When angels are assigned to a rescue operation, the assignment sometimes includes the destruction of enemies. Once, when the odds were impossibly steep against Hezekiah and the Israelites, God said, "'For I will defend this city to save it for My own sake and for My servant David's sake.' Then the angel of the LORD went out and struck 185,000 in the camp of the Assyrians; and when men arose early in the morning, behold, all of these were dead" (Isa. 37:35–36; see also 2 Kings 19:34–35).

Angels are also helping when individual people are being delivered from evil spirits. Here's a current-day example of what I'm talking about:

> In [a] service where miracles were taking place, a young man who was about twenty-five years old came into the service crying. He had a wild and desperate look on his face. You could tell he had been drinking and was high on drugs. He said to me [the woman

evangelist], "please, please help me. Won't someone help me? I want to be delivered so badly. I'm tired of this life. I'm tired of this addiction. Help me. Help me!"

The compassion of the Lord swept over the room. Filled with this compassion, we began to pray for the young man and to cast out evil spirits from him in Jesus' name. We anointed him with oil. Then we led him in the sinner's prayer, and immediately he began to shake his head. He was totally set free; when he stood up, his eyes were completely clear. This young man raised his hands in the air. Soon, he began to magnify and praise the Lord. God had totally transformed him in about fifteen minutes!

Then a little twelve-year-old boy came over and said to him, "Can I tell you something? Do you know what I saw as the people were praying for you?"

The man answered, "No."

"I saw when the demons left you, and they were standing around, trying to go back into you. But all the people were around you, praying. Then I saw an angel with a sword come and chase them away. They couldn't come back!"

The young man praised the Lord, and we were so happy that God had reached out and saved and delivered him. This man is now with good Christian people and is going to church.[6]

Angels releasing healing

Last but certainly not least, angels are assigned to release healing. The obvious scriptural illustration of angels releasing healing is found in the story of the pool of Bethesda, even though an angel does not show up in the story itself, because Jesus Himself stepped forward to release healing to a man who had been crippled for thirty-eight years. (See John 5.)

But you will remember how the story begins:

Now there is in Jerusalem a pool near the Sheep Gate. This pool in the Hebrew is called Bethesda, having five porches (alcoves, colonnades, doorways). In these lay a great number of sick folk—some blind, some crippled, and some paralyzed (shriveled up)—waiting for the bubbling up of the water. For an angel of the Lord went down at appointed seasons into the pool and moved and stirred up the water; whoever then first, after the stirring up of the water, stepped in was cured of whatever disease with which he was afflicted.

—John 5:2–4, AMP

The sick people had what some might call a folk belief (but probably it was true) that when a particular angel came, you could tell because the water of the pool, which was otherwise perfectly smooth, would move. Then, and only then, the first person into the water would be healed. It must have happened often enough to draw all of those needy people to camp out next to the pool day after day after day in hopes of being the next candidate for healing. It must have been some angel's particular assignment to go, at God's bidding, to stir the waters and release His healing power.

In our day, an angel was involved in establishing the extensive healing ministry of William M. Branham, whose ministry triggered the 1946–1956 Latter Rain movement. The account of Branham's angelic visitation on May 7, 1946, has been well documented:

> The angel said to Branham, "Fear not. I am sent from the Presence of Almighty God to tell you that your peculiar life and your misunderstood ways have been to indicate that God has sent you to take a gift of divine healing to the peoples of the world. If you will be sincere and get the people to believe you, nothing shall stand before your prayer...not even cancer!"
>
> The angel went on to tell William Branham that he would take the ministry of healing around the world and eventually pray for kings, princes and monarchs. Brother Branham responded by saying, "how [*sic*] can this be since I am a poor man and I live among poor people and I have no education." The angel then continued the commission saying, "as [*sic*] the prophet Moses was given two signs to prove that he was sent from God, so will you be given two signs."

For approximately 30 minutes the angel stood before Bro. Branham explaining the commission and the way the ministry would operate in the supernatural arena.[7]

The angel connected what was happening with what happened to Moses. The outworking of the experience connected Moses and Branham even more clearly, in that both angel-commissioned ministries were characterized by signs and wonders (including amazing healings) and deliverance.

Angels Worshiping, Watching, Working

After reading this chapter, it should be obvious to you that it's never just "Jesus and me." Angels are an essential part of the interchange between God and His people. Isn't it good to know that God has provided angels to watch over us and give us their direction and protection?

> *God, what You did before, You can do again. So we welcome Your angels to release Your manifest presence, to deliver Your word, to release revelation and understanding. Send angelic assistance to perform Your words of healing and deliverance. May angels become our hedge of protection as we serve You here on the earth, and may they usher us into Your presence when our time here is finished. Amen, in the name of Your Son, Jesus.*

I stand amazed in the presence
Of Jesus the Nazarene,
And wonder how He could love me,
A sinner, condemned, unclean.
In pity angels beheld Him,
And came from the world of light
To comfort Him in the sorrows
He bore for my soul that night.
How marvelous! How wonderful!
And my song shall ever be:
How marvelous! How wonderful
Is my Savior's love for me![1]

SEVEN

Jesus and the Ministering Angels

Throughout the Bible, wherever Jesus is, angels are there also. Angels not only announced His birth in Bethlehem, but they were also involved when individuals such as Isaiah encountered the preincarnate Christ. (See Isaiah 6:1–5.) Angels ministered to Jesus throughout His years in Palestine. They came to Him in the Garden of Gethsemane. They rolled away the stone at the entrance of His tomb, and they attended Him as He ascended to heaven before the awe-filled eyes of the disciples. They haven't stopped ministering to Him yet, because they will minister to Him forever.

The Bible accounts tell us that angels accompany Jesus wherever He goes. That means that we can expect angelic encounters when we encounter Jesus today. When we recognize that angels are near, often the next thing we're aware of is His holy presence. Jesus becomes the focus, not the angels. They simply point to Him as they serve Him.

In this chapter, I want to take a look at a number of the scriptural accounts that show us both Jesus and the ministering angels that attend Him.

Worshiping the Preincarnate Christ

In discussing Jesus and the ministering angels, you would think we would start at His birth in Bethlehem. But we can't start there, because Jesus existed long before He ever became the Incarnate One. We read in John 1:14 that "the Word became flesh, and dwelt among us." But that Word already existed before He put on human form.

Imagine what was going on in heaven before there was an Adam or an Eve, before there was a Moses, before there was an Abraham, an Isaiah, a Daniel, a Nehemiah, or a Deborah. It's the same thing that's going on today—angels surrounding God and splitting the heavens with their cries, "Holy, holy, holy is the Lord God Almighty." And where is Jesus? He's in the bosom of the Father; they are one. He was and is enthroned together with His Father. From the beginning of time, where Jesus was and is, the angels have been and still are.

"His train filled the temple"

The prophet Isaiah didn't know Jesus by name, but he got a glimpse of the angels around His throne, and it nearly wiped him out. Here was Isaiah, approximately 740 years before the birth of Jesus at Bethlehem, worshiping in the temple. King Uzziah had just died, so possibly Isaiah was there mourning his death.

Suddenly, he was caught up in a heavenly visitation. Angels appeared. Before long, his total attention was on the One who was "high and lifted up" and whose glory filled the temple. He saw the burning seraphs who, even though they themselves were fiery bright, seemed to be hiding themselves from the radiant piercing presence of God's "unapproachable light" (1 Tim. 6:16). What he saw—and heard and smelled—turned out to be almost impossible to describe, and he was appalled to recognize that he was "a man of unclean lips," completely unworthy to be in such a place, "for my eyes have seen the King, the LORD of hosts" (Isa. 6:5).

Then an amazing thing happened. A seraph who had been ministering to God in worship came and ministered to Isaiah for a moment: "Then one of the seraphim flew to me with a burning coal in his hand, which he had taken from the altar with tongs. He touched my mouth with it and said, 'Behold, this has touched your lips; and your iniquity is taken away and your sin is forgiven'" (vv. 6–7).

At this, Isaiah was able to get a grip on himself so that he could hear what the preincarnate Lord said to him: "Then I heard the voice of the Lord, saying, 'Whom shall I send, and who will go for Us?' Then I said, 'Here am I. Send me!' He said, 'Go, and tell this people…'" (vv. 8–9). The Lord Himself commissioned Isaiah to prophesy to the nation (and, by extension, to anyone who would ever read his words).

We don't know how Isaiah's temple experience ended. Surely the rest of his long and eventful life was anticlimactic compared to this one encounter with angels and with the Lord of Hosts Himself, whom he had seen with his own eyes.

"Be it unto me according to thy word"

Moments before Jesus was conceived in Mary's womb, the angel Gabriel appeared before her startled eyes. "Hail," he greeted her, "thou that art highly favoured, the Lord is with thee: blessed art thou among women" (Luke 1:28, KJV).

Gabriel reassured Mary that she would be all right and that this wasn't some kind of a mistake. He told her that she, little insignificant teenager that she was, had been selected as the one who would bear the incarnate Son of God, the Savior of the world, the King of kings.

"'How will this be,' Mary asked the angel, 'since I am a virgin?' The angel answered, 'The Holy Spirit will come upon you, and the power of the Most High will overshadow you. So the holy one to be born will be called the Son of God'" (vv. 34–35, NIV).

Then, after telling her about her older cousin Elizabeth, who had also become pregnant in a miraculous way, Gabriel stayed just a moment longer in order to hear Mary's humble response, "Behold the handmaid of the Lord; be it unto me according to thy word" (Luke 1:38, KJV). At that, Gabriel disappeared. And everything happened as he had said it would.

Gabriel, the foremost archangel, had just come to usher in the holy presence of Jesus's Spirit. This was a completely unparalleled moment in time. The angel came to Mary, ministering not only to her but also to her about-to-become-incarnate Son.

More Angelic Proclamations of His Birth

All right, now we can turn to the familiar stories of angels attending Jesus's birth. What I want you to keep seeing throughout the Bible is the connection: *wherever Jesus is, angels are there also.*

> And there were in the same country shepherds abiding in the field, keeping watch over their flock by night. And, lo, the angel of the Lord came upon them, and the glory of the Lord shone round about them: and they were sore afraid. And the angel said unto them, Fear not: for, behold, I bring you good tidings of great joy, which shall be to all people. For unto you is born this day in the city of David a Saviour, which is Christ the Lord. And this shall be a sign unto you; Ye shall find the babe wrapped in swaddling clothes, lying in a manger. And suddenly there was with the angel a multitude of the heavenly host praising God, and saying, Glory to God in the highest, and on earth peace, good will toward men.
>
> —Luke 2:8–14, KJV

More hymns have been written about this one angelic encounter than about any other. You can page through the Christmas section of a hymnbook or just recall some of the words: "Angels we have heard on high, sweetly singing o'er the plains...,"[2] "Angels, from the realms of glory, wing your flight o'er all the earth...,"[3] "While shepherds watched their flocks by night, all seated on the ground, the angel of the Lord came down, and glory shown around...,"[4] "Hark! the herald angels sing, 'Glory to the newborn King....'"[5]

Angels were everywhere to announce the arrival of the newborn Son of God, Jesus.

Faithful Joseph

Remember also that angels had visited Mary's fiancé, Joseph, in connection with the upcoming birth of Jesus. The angels spoke to him in the context of a dream.

> Because Joseph her husband was a righteous man and did not want to expose her to public disgrace, he had in mind to divorce her quietly.
>
> But after he had considered this, an angel of the Lord appeared to him in a dream and said, "Joseph son of David, do not be afraid to take Mary home as your wife, because what is conceived in her is from the Holy Spirit. She will give birth to a son, and you are to give him the name Jesus, because he will save his people from their sins."...
>
> When Joseph woke up, he did what the angel of the Lord had commanded him and took Mary home as his wife. But he had no union with her until she gave birth to a son. And he gave him the name Jesus.
>
> —Matthew 1:19–21, 24–25, NIV

This was just the first time Joseph became aware of the ministry of the angels to Mary's yet-to-be-born Son Jesus. As he would find out, the ministry of the angels would extend to all those who mattered to Jesus, including His earthly father and mother and His future disciples in the centuries yet to come.

Ministering to Jesus on Earth

Immediately after Jesus was born, angels started attending to the next part of their assignment, which was to keep Him safe for each step of His thirty-three-year-long earthly journey.

One of the first things one of them had to do was to tell Joseph (again, in a dream) to take the child and His mother to Egypt, where they would be safe from Herod's murderous rage. Joseph's obedience to the angel's instructions also fulfilled the prophetic word (see Hosea 11:1

and Numbers 24:8) that stated, "Out of Egypt have I called my son" (Matt. 2:15, KJV). Over the next months and years, it took at least a couple more angelic dream visitations to get Joseph and his family back to Israel from Egypt and then back to their hometown, Nazareth (also in fulfillment of Old Testament prophecy).

Angels in the wilderness

Matthew tells us that after Jesus was baptized, He was tested and tempted by satan in the wilderness. After a month and a half of hungry days, the angels showed up to minister to Him. "Then the devil left Him; and behold, angels came and began to minister to Him" (Matt. 4:11; see also Mark 1:13).

The Greek word that is translated "minister" in English is *diakoneo*. From that word comes our English word *deacon*. That means that angels are heaven's deacons. They provide very practical services. They came to give Jesus nourishment, rest, and strength after His bouts with the devil in the wilderness, and likewise, they render their caring services to those of us who bear Jesus's Spirit today.

They come to minister to those who inherit salvation. (See Hebrews 1:14.) Angels are heaven's deacons—isn't that good?

Angels supplying strength in Gethsemane

Fast-forwarding to the end of Jesus's three years as an itinerant rabbi, we see an angel coming to minister to Jesus at one of the most critical junctures of His life.

Jesus really needed angelic help in the Garden of Gethsemane. When the Son of God is literally sweating blood, you know that even He has no more resources left. The disciples who had come along with Him couldn't do anything for Him, because they had fallen asleep.

So, coming with somber strength, "there appeared to Him an angel from heaven, strengthening Him in spirit" (Luke 22:43, AMP).

The end and the beginning

Then the disciples woke up. There came their fellow disciple Judas, leading a mob of chief priests and elders who had come to arrest Jesus.

Frantic, Peter grabbed his sword and swung it at their foes, cutting off a slave's ear.

Here, the interesting thing is that angels did *not* arrive in force to defend Jesus. They certainly could have. But they were not summoned to do so. This was Jesus's time. He had to be arrested, flogged, and crucified. As He was being arrested, Jesus mentioned the angels:

> Then Jesus said to him, Put your sword back into its place, for all who draw the sword will die by the sword. Do you suppose that I cannot appeal to My Father, and He will immediately provide Me with more than twelve legions [more than 80,000] of angels? But how then would the Scriptures be fulfilled, that it must come about this way?
>
> —Matthew 26:52–54, AMP

See how obedient the angels are? If one of us had been there, we might have been more like Peter, rushing in "where angels fear to tread." Angels are watchers. They watch and wait—and they move very swiftly when they are summoned, especially if they are being summoned by the Son of God Himself.

Angels Serving at the Resurrection and Ascension of Jesus

After the death of Jesus, angels started appearing to believers. Every appearance shows us how they serve and minister—announcing, explaining, and guiding the way to the One whom death could not hold.

The two Marys, in deep grief, were the first ones to encounter an angel:

> Now after the Sabbath, near dawn of the first day of the week, Mary of Magdala and the other Mary went to take a look at the tomb. And behold, there was a great earthquake, for an angel of the Lord descended from heaven and came and rolled the boulder back and sat upon it. His appearance was like lightning, and his garments as

white as snow. And those keeping guard were so frightened at the sight of him that they were agitated and they trembled and became like dead men. But the angel said to the women, Do not be alarmed and frightened, for I know that you are looking for Jesus, Who was crucified. He is not here; He has risen, as He said [He would do]. Come, see the place where He lay. Then go quickly and tell His disciples, He has risen from the dead, and behold, He is going before you to Galilee; there you will see Him. Behold, I have told you. So they left the tomb hastily with fear and great joy and ran to tell the disciples. And as they went, behold, Jesus met them and said, Hail (greetings)! And they went up to Him and clasped His feet and worshiped Him.

—Matthew 28:1–9, AMP

Over the next days, after appearing Himself multiple times to the astonished believers, Jesus left them with these words—and another glimpse of His attending angels:

"But you will receive power when the Holy Spirit has come upon you; and you shall be My witnesses both in Jerusalem, and in all Judea and Samaria, and even to the remotest part of the earth."

And after He had said these things, He was lifted up while they were looking on, and a cloud received Him out of their sight. And as they were gazing intently into the sky while He was going, behold, two men in white clothing stood beside them. They also said, "Men of Galilee, why do you stand looking into the sky? This Jesus, who has been taken up from you into heaven, will come in just the same way as you have watched Him go into heaven."

—Acts 1:8–11

Descending at the Second Coming

All of that leads us to all the verses and passages of Scripture that form our expectations for the future return of the Lord Jesus Christ. Here's a quick sampling of them. Jesus Himself is speaking in the first two:

For the Son of Man is going to come in the glory of His Father with His angels.

—Matthew 16:27

But when the Son of Man comes in His glory, and all the angels with Him, then He will sit on His glorious throne.

—Matthew 25:31

For after all it is only just for God to repay with affliction those who afflict you, and to give relief to you who are afflicted and to us as well *when the Lord Jesus will be revealed from heaven with His mighty angels in flaming fire*, dealing out retribution to those who do not know God and to those who do not obey the gospel of our Lord Jesus.

—2 Thessalonians 1:6–8, emphasis added

In addition to these, I want to quote a choice passage in which Jesus pulls back the veil for a moment. He has just met Nathanael:

Nathanael answered Him, "Rabbi, You are the Son of God; You are the King of Israel."

Jesus answered and said to him, "Because I said to you that I saw you under the fig tree, do you believe? You will see greater things than these." And He said to him, "Truly, truly, I say to you, you will see the heavens opened and the angels of God ascending and descending on the Son of Man."

—John 1:49–51

I want to be a Nathanael, don't you? I want to see that!

Exalting Christ Forever

After Jesus comes again, we will be only one short step from joining the angels in their eternal ministry of worship, the finest and highest ministry of all. Exalting the Lamb of God, Jesus Christ, forever and ever—what a magnificent future awaits us!

Then I [John] looked, and I heard the voice of many angels around the throne and the living creatures and the elders; and the number of them was myriads of myriads, and thousands of thousands, saying with a loud voice, "Worthy is the Lamb that was slain to receive power and riches and wisdom and might and honor and glory and blessing." And every created thing which is in heaven and on the earth and under the earth and on the sea, and all things in them, I heard saying, "To Him who sits on the throne, and to the Lamb, be blessing and honor and glory and dominion forever and ever." And the four living creatures kept saying, "Amen." And the elders fell down and worshiped.

—Revelation 5:11–14

Jesus, with the angels, we worship You. You have captured our hearts, and You are altogether lovely. Jesus, the bright and morning star, Lamb of God, Son of God, Messiah, Savior, King, Holy One. With all of the radiant angels who surround You, we cry, "Holy, holy, holy..." and we say we love You better than anything else.

It came upon a midnight clear,
That glorious song of old,
From angels bending near the earth,
To touch their harps of gold:
"Peace on the earth, good will to men,
From heav'n's all-gracious King."
The world in solemn stillness lay,
To hear the angels sing.
Still through the cloven skies they come,
With peaceful wings unfurled,
And still their heavenly music floats
O'er all the weary world;
Above its sad and lowly plains,
They bend on hovering wing,
And ever o'er its Babel sounds
The blessed angels sing.[1]

EIGHT

Modern-Day Reports of Angelic Encounters

(by Michal Ann Goll)

D o you realize that right this minute, as you are reading this book, you may have an angel within arm's reach? It's so much easier to pay attention to the natural world than it is to the unseen heavenly realm, even though both are all around us all of the time.

In this chapter, I want to raise your awareness to a new level by presenting a number of stories from the lives of ordinary people who have experienced angelic intervention. When you hear about different ways that angels have worked, you can become more open to the wide range of "options" that are out there. God really does seem to enjoy variety. He has filled the world—both the natural world we know so well and the unseen supernatural world—with an awesome amount of diversity. The angelic realm is no exception.

Angels can show up anywhere, and they can assume whatever appearance they need to take on. They can touch you or shake your hand, and they can disappear into thin air. They come at God's bidding, but you can't predict their coming. In these stories, you will see that some of the people who encountered angels were in desperate straits. Some of them weren't. Often the people didn't know angels had been involved until later, but when they tried to figure out what had happened, they couldn't explain it any other way.

To start off, let me tell you about what happened to our friend Betsy Headden, who, not long ago, received what must have been some angelic assistance. She wasn't desperate—in fact, she had been sailing along the highway worshiping God and without a care in the world—and God sent her help before she even asked for it. Here's her story, in her words:

I had driven from my home in Nashville, Tennessee, to Macon, Georgia, to visit my first cousin, who had been diagnosed with terminal cancer and with whom I had been very close when we were growing up. I had felt that God wanted me to pray with her for healing and also to talk to her about the Lord if she turned out not to be saved. On the way to her house, I stopped in Atlanta, Georgia, to spend the night with my favorite aunt and uncle, who were in their early eighties. I knew that they did not know the Lord in a personal way, and I had prayed for an opening to share with them about Him. Much prayer had gone into this trip.

Now I was on my way home, rejoicing after an incredible time with each family member. The Lord had opened the door wide for me to share with my aunt and uncle. And in Macon, I had found that my cousin was a brand-new, very strong believer, and we had had a powerful time of prayer together.

As I drove home, I was somewhat baffled to discover that what had been a two-hour drive earlier had taken me only forty-five minutes in this direction, driving the same speed in the same kind of traffic. I must have had supernatural assistance. Little did I know I was about to receive some more!

I was driving homeward on the interstate in my car, singing God's praises along with a worship CD, one hand raised high and the other on the wheel. I was soaring in the Spirit. All of a sudden, I noticed that my car was slowing down. I looked at the gas gauge, and there it was, showing completely empty. I just happened to be near enough to an exit ramp to coast over to it. There was a long line of backed-up traffic already on this exit, and the line moved only when the light ahead changed. There were a few other cars behind me and many in front of me. What was I to do?

Before I even had time to think or pray, I saw two men get out of their car, which was two cars ahead of mine, and walk back to my car. They came to my window and said to me, "Do you need some gasoline?" One of them had a five-gallon can of gas in his hand!

I said yes, and they poured it into my gas tank in a few seconds. I tried to pay them, but they refused payment. They told me where I could find a gas station near the exit so I could go and fill up.

There was no way any mere men could have known that I was out of gas. I was one of twenty-five cars standing still in a line of cars. I had only been sitting there for two or three seconds before they appeared at my window. They looked to be in their mid- to late-thirties, and they were wearing blue jeans. They had a light about their faces and very kind smiles. There is only one possible explanation—they were angels.

As you can see, Betsy didn't do anything special to attract angelic road service. She was just going about God's business, faithfully and prayerfully. She did notice something a little different about the two men, even though they looked pretty "normal" for the situation. They came, they accomplished what was important, and they left, and Betsy went on her way, praising God even more than before.

We see that angels can take on any human form, usually blending in with the kind of people who are in a particular location. And they offer just the right type and amount of help, offering it in a decisive and clear manner.

An Extra Measure

Leon and Paula Hoover have been partnering with our ministry for a few years, but before they came to Tennessee, they served as missionaries in West Africa. While they were there, they experienced a time of great trials. For the sake of brevity, I will condense his account in the following pages.

Leon and his daughter, Natalie, had fallen very sick, and yet he and Paula tried to keep up with their duties. They also had a young son named Luke. Because of the sickness, the family was having difficulty sleeping through the night, all in one room of their little house. In Leon's words:

> We had learned early on in our stay that visiting the sick is an important part of life in West Africa. Our house had been crowded with people wanting to simply *be* with me during my sickness.
>
> After the evening chores, most of which were done by Paula, we again quickly made our rounds among the huts to excuse ourselves for not sitting around their fire and sharing their food. They were always so gracious, but we could tell they felt badly for us.
>
> That night, we did sleep. I awoke very peacefully around 4:00 a.m. Realizing we had all been asleep since well before midnight, I began thanking Jesus for His faithfulness and for this precious gift of peaceful rest. I was so grateful. As I prayed, I drifted off into a deep sleep again. So it was that I didn't really see or hear him come in....
>
> Groggy from my first peaceful night's rest, I couldn't quite understand what was going on. *Who was this, and what did he want that couldn't wait until the sun was up?*
>
> The inside of our mud brick home was as dark as a cave during the night. With the window and door shut to keep out the bats, I could hardly see my hand in front of my face. But behind him, the tin door to the exterior hung ajar on its hinges, so that the moonlight drifted inside to outline his silhouette. Sitting there on his heels, he filled the width and a good portion of the five-foot-high doorway into our sleeping chamber. Otherwise, I might not have seen him at all.
>
> He was big, bigger than the men I had seen at Yenderé. Yet he was dressed much like them, wearing a tattered sleeveless shirt and pants, much like the ones used when working in the fields. He was squatting quietly on his heels at the foot of our cots. Breathing rapidly like an athlete after a track event, he seemed winded, though not tired. I was not surprised by that; all the men around there were

in excellent physical condition. It seemed he had traveled a great distance or had hurried to get here. *But why?*

"It's good you're sleeping well," he said.

"Yes, I'm very grateful," I replied.

In his big brown hands, he held a large gourd bowl. I had seen it when I realized he was in the hut. In the back of my mind, I hoped it wasn't full of that corn flour drink. But I figured if he had bothered to come at this hour of the morning, I ought to be polite enough to accept whatever he offered.

He produced a large metal spoon. I couldn't really see from where; perhaps it had been inside his open shirt. As he slowly stirred the contents of the bowl, I began to wake up enough to wonder just what was going on. *Who was this guy?* He was huge, and I didn't recognize him as being part of the village. My eyes had adjusted enough to discern the definition of his muscles. His breathing rate had already slowed. It was nearly back to normal, and he seemed so pleased.... *Why was that?* But he was saying something else. *What was it?*

"We were on our way from the beginning, but there was some trouble. It was..."

"You mean there was a fight?" I interrupted. "A fight? Then you must..."

"Merely a delay," he continued. "There was some opposition to our coming, but that's settled. We're here now, and that's why you sleep well."

When I first saw him, I had wondered why his presence had not startled me. Now, however, it was apparent whose messenger he was. I knew that whatever he had in that bowl for me, I should accept. No more words were needed. He dipped the spoon into the bowl and held it to my mouth. I swallowed it all. Though it seemed a familiar substance, it was rather like nothing at all going down. There wasn't much taste and not much to say about its consistency either. I couldn't place it. I was relieved, though, and glad to have taken my spoonful.

I awoke Paula, Luke, and Natalie, telling them they needed to take a spoonful of this. We were all sitting cross-legged on our cots in a semicircle around the visitor squatting in the doorway. I was concerned that Luke and Natalie might not take the drink. "Each of you need to take this," I said. He gave each of them a spoonful, dipping into the gourd and putting the spoon to their lips just as he had for me. I watched them lie down again, and when I turned toward the door, he was gone. He had gone out as quietly and peacefully as he had come in.

It was around 5:30 before I awoke again. As the morning light slipped under the edges of the straw roof, I could hear the village coming to life. I lay there pondering the experience. I had never been visited by an angel, much less talked with one. *Had it been more than a dream? Had I been awake? And that bowl, what exactly had he given us?*

Luke, Natalie, and Paula awoke soon. As they were getting dressed, I sat on my cot and recounted to Luke the angel's coming, as Natalie and Paula listened closely. It was during the retelling of it that I realized what he had given us.

Leon goes on to recount how his condition and Natalie's grew worse as the day went on. Thanks to the loan of a moped, all four of them were able to reach a medical clinic in a bigger town, and, through a series of God-ordained "coincidences," eventually to a mission hospital in the neighboring country of Cote d'Ivoire. Leon and Natalie seemed to be suffering from malaria.

Even with medical treatment, Leon's condition grew so serious that "death did not seem a remote possibility." So early one morning in the hospital, he set his spiritual house in order, writing individual letters to his wife and the two children, adding one for the unborn child that he and Paula suspected she was carrying. He tucked the letters into his Bible.

Within a week, however, he was well enough to return to them, although he was weak and had lost more than twenty-five pounds. So Leon and Paula kept taking care of their family and working. (They were in training as missionaries.) Over time, Leon suffered several relapses. Finally, medical personnel decided that he must be fighting more than malaria, and tests in another hospital in Lomé revealed hepatitis B as well as typhoid fever and a severe infestation of giardia. He had to stay in Lomé for nearly three months, with most of it on complete bed rest. This was very difficult indeed on the whole family. On top of everything else, Paula did turn out to be pregnant, but she lost the baby, most likely because of the anti-malaria drugs she had been taking. They clung to their faith in God, and He kept them from sinking into complete discouragement.

What had been in the bowl? What had the angel given them to drink? Leon writes:

> The bowl the angel had brought us was full of *faith*, "the substance of things hoped for, the evidence of things not seen" [Heb. 11:1, KJV]. The angel had been sent to give us each an extra measure of faith....
>
> We surely needed that extra measure of faith, because ours was running low. The light within us had grown dim; the beast of impossibility was ready to take us. Somehow though, with God's grace, we managed to [put] that behind us.
>
> God's grace. The fear of the Lord. Those were household expressions for us back in Georgia [in the States, before they came to Africa]. Now we tremble with respect, adoration, and love at the thought of the awesome and holy God we serve.

The angel provided *faith*, which was exactly what the Hoovers needed. Once he had delivered that, they used their extra measure of faith to get through that difficult season and, even as they do now, to continue to step over impossibilities.

Angels in Ravensbrück

As Leon and Paula learned, angels most often come to provide miraculous assistance, but they do not completely eliminate the difficulties that made their help necessary. Our own faith must play a big role. This was also the experience of Corrie ten Boom, a Dutch woman who was arrested by the Nazis during World War II for hiding Jews and who became famous later in her life because of her book and a film, both called *The Hiding Place*.

Corrie and her sister Betsie were transferred from a concentration camp in the Netherlands to the infamous Ravensbrück camp in Germany. After they had been unloaded from the train that had brought them to Germany, they were being processed, herded like cattle, along with a crowd of women prisoners. Corrie tells what happened:

Together we entered the terrifying building. At a table were women who took away all our possessions. Everyone had to undress completely and then go to a room where her hair was checked.

I asked a woman who was busy checking the possessions of the new arrivals if I might use the toilet. She pointed to a door, and I discovered that the convenience was nothing more than a hole in the shower room floor. Betsie stayed close beside me all the time. Suddenly I had an inspiration, "Quick, take off your woolen underwear," I whispered to her. I rolled it up with mine and laid the bundle in a corner with my little Bible. The spot was alive with cockroaches, but I didn't worry about that. I felt wonderfully relieved and happy....

We hurried back to the row of women waiting to be undressed. A little later, after we had had our showers and put on our shirts and shabby dresses, I hid the roll of underwear and my Bible under my dress. It did bulge out obviously through my dress; but I prayed, "Lord, cause now Thine angels to surround me; and let them not be transparent today, for the guards must not see me." I felt perfectly at ease. Calmly I passed the guards. Everyone was checked, from the front, the sides, the back. Not a bulge escaped the eyes of the guard. The woman just in front of me had hidden a woolen vest under her dress; it was taken from her. They let me pass, for they did not see me. Betsie, right behind me, was searched.

But outside awaited another danger. On each side of the door were women who looked everyone over for a second time. They felt over the body of each one who passed. I knew they would not see me, for the angels were still surrounding me. I was not even surprised when they passed me by; but within me rose the jubilant cry, "O Lord, if Thou dost so answer prayer, I can face even Ravensbrück unafraid."[2]

This story appears in Billy Graham's book *Angels: God's Secret Agents,* which is a great source of information about angels. Graham also tells a story that was told to him when he was visiting American troops during the Korean War. It happened to a group of marines in the First Division, who were stranded in what is now North Korea during bitter winter weather. The temperature went down to 20 degrees below zero, and the men were in desperate straits. Besides nearly freezing to death, they had not eaten in six days. One of the men was a Christian, and he encouraged the others to praise God in the midst of their situation. Suddenly, they were startled by the crashing of a wild boar rushing toward them. They scrambled out of his way, and one of the soldiers aimed his rifle to shoot. But before he could (which might have betrayed their location to the enemy), the boar simply toppled over, dead. They feasted that night on fresh meat, and they regained their strength.

The next day, they heard another noise, and of course they feared that it was an enemy patrol. But inexplicably, it was a South Korean who could speak English, and he said, "I will show you out." He led them through the mountain forests until they reached the safety of their own territory. And—just to underline the angelic nature of the whole series of events—their nameless savior disappeared before they could thank him.[3]

Super-Sized Angels

In Corrie ten Boom's situation, nobody saw the angels involved—but the guards didn't see *her,* either, which proved that she had been shielded from their scrutiny. In Leon's and Betsy's situations, as well as the marines' situation in Korea, the angels looked like ordinary "good Samaritans," people who could blend in with the others around them.

But Joel Staab, another friend of ours, saw an angel who definitely did *not* blend in with the crowd:

> I had come up for prayer after a special speaker had been sharing at our church. Right after the speaker prayed for me, I felt a very strong presence of what I thought was the Holy Spirit, and may have been, but as I opened my eyes, I had a somewhat open vision: I saw this *massive* foot there. It looked to be a good forty feet long. My eyes followed it up and up, and I realized I was looking at an angel of gigantic proportions.
>
> I have to add that although it was a seemingly open vision, I could not see the angel in any detail; in fact, it almost appeared comic-book-like in nature, which made it hard to decide what I was seeing. It looked to be hundreds of feet tall.
>
> I stared, looking straight up. His face was kindly, almost boyish, kind of full, and my thoughts were, *Why would God have an angel this big?*
>
> It was as if the angel heard me, because he answered, "It takes big angels to move mountains!" He smiled, and then the vision ended.

Joel didn't know whether his angel encounter was an open vision (seeing a physical reality with your physical eyes) or not. He might have been seeing with both his physical eyes and his spiritual sight at the same time. But you know what? It didn't matter. It was a real angel, and it had a real message for him—and, by extension, for those of us who have heard about what he saw and heard.

It really doesn't matter whether we perceive angels through waking visions, dreams (which are visions when you're sleeping), or in person. What matters is the result of their visitation. It doesn't matter if they come briefly (which seems to be most common) or for a prolonged period of time. What matters is that they are able to bring us strength, protection, courage, faith, or whatever else God knows that we need.

Two Visits, Twenty Years Apart

In chapter 5, I mentioned Roland Buck, who wrote a book called *Angels on Assignment*. He included the story of a man named John Weaver, who was visited by the same angel twice, under completely different circumstances:

> As I was fixing my car alongside the road, I saw a car coming right across the plowed field about a quarter of a mile from me. It was a brand-new car, and the dirt and dust were flying behind it as it came right across the plowed field at me. He drove me into town so I could secure help and then instantly disappeared. I learned later that it was an angel coming to my rescue.
>
> God visited me in a very special way again in 1971 and spoke to me about the work I was to do for Him. At this point in time in my ministry and my spiritual development, God in His grace saw fit to send the same angel to speak to me once again who had helped me approximately twenty years earlier.
>
> It was wintertime in Montana, and some friends and I went hunting for elk. I was two-thirds of the way to the top of the ridge where I was headed when I saw a man coming out of the trees on the next ridge near the timberline. He did not have on hunter orange and he was walking right down to me without carrying a gun. He seemed to be walking at the same pace a normal man would walk, but he covered the ground between us so quickly... in a matter of seconds! I noticed that as he walked, *he left no footprints in the snow!*
>
> The man walked up to me and shook my hand. He said, "John, do you know who I am?"
>
> I responded, speaking out of my spirit, "Yes, you are a servant of the Lord."
>
> He said, "Yes, that is right. The Lord has sent me here today to talk with you." We sat down on two big rocks facing each other. It was not until later that I realized I was talking with the same angel who had helped me when my car broke down twenty years earlier!

We talked about how God was pleased that I had moved my prayer life from a selfish prayer to one of compassion for those around me and, among other things, about needing a house for my family...at that point the angel stopped me! This was the first time he had said anything since I had begun sharing with him. He said, "How much money do you need?"

I said, "Maybe $20,000."

The angel said, "You know that I could give you that $20,000 in hundred-dollar bills right now, don't you?" Somehow I knew he could do it, so I replied, "Yes." He said, "We don't do things that way, though. The Lord puts it upon the hearts of His people. That money will be taken care of and you don't have to tell anyone. It will just come in." He talked with me twenty or thirty minutes more, telling me some beautiful truths and some exciting things about how it would be in eternity in heaven. What a thrill!...

Two weeks later, I was driving back from a meeting, worshiping the Lord in the car and thinking about the $20,000 the angel had mentioned. Suddenly, I felt the Lord's presence in the car right beside me. Whether it was the angel again speaking for the Lord or the Lord speaking directly, I do not know. He spoke to me about the $20,000, reminding me that I had never asked for it. When I replied by asking, He said, "Starting tomorrow morning, that money is going to come in." And just like that, it was as though he slipped out of the moving car and was gone.[4]

Dreaming About Angels

We're beginning to see the pattern—the important thing is the fact that angels really do come to help us, not how they come or exactly what they do. If you, like John Weaver, encounter an angel who shakes your hand and then sits down across from you to have a long conversation, that's wonderful. If you see a vision of a forty-foot-long *foot* in front of you and discover that it belongs to an angel who is taller than a house, that's wonderful, too.

And if you don't see anything with your physical eyes because you end up dreaming about an angelic encounter, that's every bit as wonderful. Read what Sandie Freed (a prophetic minister from Texas) learned about the importance of angels in dreams:

> It is through dreams that God often speaks to us. In fact, God saved His Son through a dream. Remember Joseph, the earthly father of Jesus, was told in a *dream* about the birth of Jesus, and also received warnings concerning Jesus' safety. In the dreams, Joseph was instructed where to move Jesus for protection....
>
> I have made the mistake of not feeling that dreams of angels were as important as actually "seeing" them with the natural eye. I actually complained to the Lord that I only "dreamed" of angels, and I wanted to actually "see" angels. Then one day, the Lord rebuked me and said, "Well, if a dream with an angel was important enough to save my only Son, a dream with an angel is also good enough for you!"
>
> Wow! Talk about falling on your knees and repenting! So now, whenever I have a dream about angels, I take it very seriously. As far as God is concerned, dreaming of angels is just as important as a vision, or actually seeing them....
>
> In Genesis 28, the Scripture tells us about Jacob who...lay down to sleep. In a dream, a ladder appeared....There were angels of God that ascended and descended on the ladder....The Lord stood above the ladder and made a prophetic declaration to Jacob that He was going to bless Jacob's seed. Actually, a covenant promise was made by God to Jacob during this dream.
>
> ...How important our dreams are! God may be releasing covenant promises to us while we sleep![5]

Angels in the Labor Room

Now, just to balance out what I just quoted about angels appearing in dreams, here's a true story from another friend of ours, Susie Roye, who was visited in person by seven strong angels while she was in active labor with her third child:

The most personally significant angelic encounter I've had occurred while I was in labor with our third baby. This encounter was directly related to my previous two labors and deliveries, the first of which was extraordinarily and unnecessarily painful; this difficult experience left me with an overwhelming amount of fear associated with childbirth.

The third baby came along in another city, and God had promised me that He would deliver me this time, once and for all, from the fear and trauma of my first birth experience. To the hospital I carried with me all of Exodus 15, full of so many promises that the enemy, my "Egyptians," would be put down once and for all. This was my hope, my promise, and I was even trying to mutter Miriam's song. I was terrified otherwise.

My labor progressed, and things were not going well. The doctor was pacing and calling in advice from others. I was terrified and more terrified, while simultaneously clinging to my promises from Exodus. I had peace one second and all-out panic the next. Where was God in all of this? How could this be? And now it was not just my own battle in my heart, but things weren't looking good for my baby either. A nurse came to insert several IV tubes in my arm so they could be ready for anything I might need. She poked and poked and poked and poked some more, and could not get even one vein in my arm. I was already in a lot of pain, and now this. She called in another nurse, who poked and poked my arm, with no success. This was horrible. They switched arms, and poked some more. I was nearly going over the edge. What about the promises? I thought I had come into this knowing I would conquer my fears and past traumas. My husband Mark sat by my bed watching all this, reading his Bible and feeling helpless.

Suddenly, the atmosphere changed all around the room. At the foot of my bed stood seven angels. They actually stood against the wall, and they were at least as tall as the ceiling. They were very large, muscular, male figures; I could clearly see their very broad and muscular chests and arms. I could not clearly see their faces, but I could vaguely make out facial features and some loose, curly hair about chin-length. They were radiant head to toe, brightly glowing, enveloped in a bright, shiny, white and yellow light. As the nurses poked the second arm with a needle with no success, one angel left the wall and walked over by my bed, leaned in between the two nurses as if to see what was going on, and the needle slipped right in, painlessly. The angel then went back and stood against the wall with the others. They were fearsome-looking, but instead of acting like they were ready for a fight, they were smiling, happy, talking among themselves, and glancing toward me.

The horrible battle I had brought with me was now gone! I had a sudden realization that although these guys were huge and ready for anything, there was no longer any battle here. Instantly, everything my doctor was concerned about came into order. Things smoothed out. Then I realized that my Egyptians were really, really gone.

While the seven angels were in the labor room, Mark could not see them, but he could sense that something invisible was happening. I was transfixed on the angels while they were present. Once everything in the room was going peacefully, the angels sort of faded away right in front of my eyes. As they faded away, I could hear Mark's voice growing louder, calling my name, repeatedly asking me what was going on. Finally I was able to turn to him and tell him what had happened. Soon after, the baby was born without further incident.

A fourth baby followed two years later, and the experience was perfectly wonderful, peaceful, and in order, including labor and delivery. I feel that a huge battle was won that day, freedom from bondage to past experiences and threats to my welfare and the baby's, but the victory came without swords or screaming or rebuking. The victory came because of an overwhelming and drenching presence of God to a very feeble vessel that was more full of fear than faith. "Let God arise and His enemies be scattered" (Ps. 68:1). He did, and they were!

Susie's story is so exciting, and it raises my expectations once again that God will send His angels to help us in our times of need. It also illustrates a very important truth: where angels are, God is, and vice versa.

To the Royes, the peace of the angelic presence and the "drenching" presence of God felt the same.

Next, I want to tell you a story that will stretch you a little further; it shows how "dark angels" perceive the sweet presence of God and His angels, and how someone overheard what the devil was worried about.

"I Smell Chocolate!"

Bill Yount, whose ministry takes him from his home in Maryland to many other parts of the country, introduces the context for this prophetic word about Hershey, Pennsylvania. Hershey, as most people know, is famous because of the Hershey Chocolate Company and is named after candy maker and philanthropist Milton Hershey (1857–1945). Milton Hershey's wife, Catherine, couldn't have children, and she suffered from a deteriorating muscular disease. Her situation motivated her husband to establish a school for financially needy children, the Milton Hershey School, and to become involved in medical research. Through the Milton Hershey School Trust, a medical research hospital and medical school, now part of the University of Pennsylvania, were established. All the Hershey endeavors are flourishing to this day.

Bill Yount was in prayer about Hershey, Pennsylvania, and he overheard the messages of some angels—both fallen and unfallen ones:

> I saw one of the greatest outpourings of healing being erected as a healing zone, invading and surrounding the community at large (I do mean large!) of Hershey, PA. I heard a strong angel decreeing: "And there shall be 'drive thru' healings taking place in this city and surrounding its borders."...
>
> I heard the enemy complaining and regretting the days that the womb of Milton Hershey's wife could not conceive. "Now we have a 'womb of healing' opening up in this place, where multitudes will conceive their healing for the nations!" I heard the stronghold spirit over Hershey crying out to hell, "It's Hershey; we've got a problem!"

I saw the angels of orphans and underprivileged children standing before the face of the Father, bringing their cries of "Abba, Father," and their tears for Daddy to come home to Hershey to be with them.

I heard the Father dispatching something like a news alert back to these orphans and children, "I'll be there with bells on! I am coming to bless the day Milton Hershey blessed my orphaned, fatherless children. I am coming to bless the whole town, city, and beyond its borders!...I am turning the hearts of the children to their fathers and the hearts of the fathers to their children."...

I saw angels dropping cures for diseases into the Hershey Medical Center. Unknown sicknesses and diseases were being given names, and angels were dropping these names down, and cures were following behind them to be released to the world....

I heard the enemy proclaiming throughout all of hell: "We have been working overtime to stop those praying Christians and to bring division to those churches and families, but we have overlooked the power of the cries of the fatherless! Those cries were coming from outside of the church and ascending straight to the Throne of their real Father! And He's coming to Hershey with full force!"...

As a sweet-smelling aroma ascended from Hershey, Pennsylvania, to the throne, trembling words from hell came screaming, "I SMELL CHOCOLATE, I SMELL MILK, AND I SMELL HONEY. IT SMELLS LIKE THE PROMISED LAND!"[6]

What can you say to *that*? It seems like each angel story is more fascinating than the last.

Angels Watching Over Me

Many of the angel stories you may have heard up to this time concern angelic protection or angelic guidance. Probably we fail to appreciate the multitude of ways that angels keep us safe and on the right path.

Cindy Jacobs tells a story in her book *The Supernatural Life* that mirrors experiences others have had:

Leslyn Musch and I had just arrived in Caracas, Venezuela. As we stepped out of the airplane and into muggy night air, I said, "I sure hope that someone is here to pick us up. My Spanish is not very good." I was joking, but I was more prophetic than I knew.

It was around 9:30 p.m. and we were tired from a long day of travel. We collected our bags and headed through customs without any hassles. The doors whooshed open and we wheeled our luggage into a waiting area. Expectantly, we panned the crowd for some kind of welcoming sign or someone sent by the church to pick us up. There was no sign, nor was there a driver. We gave each other a maybe-they're-just-caught-in-traffic look.

The clock was ticking, so I decided to try out my Spanish. But everyone was leaving. To our consternation every shop started to close: the money exchange and ticket counters—everything. It happened too quickly that we didn't realize our predicament until it was too late.

We found some people and asked in our limited way if it was safe to go into the city via taxi. The people looked positively horrified and exclaimed, *"Peligro!"* That means "danger," and I understood that much. At last, after dragging our bags through more of the airport, we sat down in a conspicuous place...I said to her, "I think it's time to pray—hard!" She agreed.

It got later and later and our prayers became more fervent when a nice-looking, young, Venezuelan-appearing man wearing a suit approached us. "Hello," he cheerfully stated in perfect English, "I am here to meet VIPs. Do you need some help?"...

...I explained to the young man that we needed to call the hotel but didn't have a phone card. "No problem," he said, grinning and holding one up in the air. "I have one."

"Wonderful," I replied, and we walked around the corner to the phones, leaving Leslyn to guard the suitcases. I gave the young Venezuelan the number of the hotel, and he dialed it, talked to the front desk, and then handed the phone to me. Thankfully, the man on the other end of the line spoke English....

...While I waited for the hotel staffer to find our reservation, I glanced over at the man and thanked the Lord for him. He gave me another of those wonderful grins and said, "By the way, my name is Luis, and I am angel from God." I stared at him blankly in unbelief as I held the receiver of the phone. "You are an *angel?*" Once again the big smile, and then he pointed toward heaven and replied, "Yes, you know, from there."

Before I hung up the phone, arrangements had been made for a driver from the hotel to come pick us up. Luis and I walked back to Leslyn. I have to admit, I was in a bit of a state of shock....

I told Leslyn that a car was coming to pick us up, and when I turned around, Luis was gone. We never saw him again. The next day we found out that we had been expected at 10:00 *a.m.* rather than 10:00 *p.m.* That explained why there was no driver waiting for us. Thank God for our welcoming angel![7]

Many, many people have experienced the outright protection of angels from imminent dangers. Here is another account. This one is from Terry Law's book *The Truth About Angels,* and it's about a woman's protection during a tornado:

My encounter occurred in 1976 when we lived in Missouri. It was the wee hours of the morning, and we had been having severe weather. We lived in a mobile home, and I was very fearful of storms. I remember waking up to a loud noise outside our bedroom window that sounded like a freight train. The window was shaking, and the whole house seemed to be moving.

My husband was sound asleep next to me, but I was too scared to move or even wake him up. I began to pray fervently, asking God to spare my home and family because I knew that if He did not intervene, tragedy would hit. In that moment the Lord began to speak peace to me. I felt He wanted me to get up and look out the window so He could show me something. I eased my way up to the window and pulled open the curtains.

To my surprise and shock, I saw a very bright light and figures of tall, broad-shouldered beings dressed in long, white robes. They had strong arms and hands and were holding hands, standing with their backs to the wind and their faces toward me. However, I could not see their faces clearly because they were so bright.

At that moment I knew that angels were encompassing the mobile home and us. I sat on the bed, just gazing out of the window in awe for about fifteen minutes. All fear left, and I felt safe and secure. From that day on, whenever a storm comes my way, I know strong angels are there to protect me.[8]

Peace on Earth

This chapter is like an appetizer—it's just a small taste of the endless number of ways that people encounter angels every single day around the world. Many, many times—probably most of the time—people don't realize that angels have been involved in the events of their daily lives. But they *are*, without fanfare, simply and dependably doing God's bidding, always working to bring His kingdom to Earth in tangible ways.

We get so used to singing the words of Christmas carols that we don't notice how many of them refer to angels. Look again at the words of "It Came Upon a Midnight Clear" at the beginning of this chapter. "Still through the cloven skies they come..." "Still their heavenly music floats o'er all the weary world..." "And ever o'er its Babel sounds, the blessed angels sing." What's that sound? It's the angels—they're still bringing God's love to Earth.

> *Lord, I enter into Your rest right now, and I invite Your angelic presence to come into this place. I say, "Messengers, come. Messengers, come to do the labors for which you have been designed!" Amen.*

And though this world, with devils filled,
Should threaten to undo us,
We will not fear, for God hath willed
His truth to triumph through us:
The Prince of Darkness grim,
We tremble not for him;
His rage we can endure,
For lo, his doom is sure;
One little word shall fell him.
That word above all earthly pow'rs,
No thanks to them, abideth;
The Spirit and the gifts are ours,
Through Him who with us sideth.
Let goods and kindred go,
This mortal life also;
The body they may kill;
God's truth abideth still,
His kingdom is forever.[1]

NINE

Discerning the Angelic Presence

Have you ever seen or felt an angelic presence—or a demonic one? When we "see" or "sense" or "feel" a spiritual entity nearby, we have *discerned* its presence. This chapter is devoted to the topic of discerning the angelic presence because it's vital to be able to distinguish spiritual origins and outcomes when you're dealing with supernatural realities. Both good and bad (fallen) angels are spiritual beings, and we need the gift of discerning of spirits when we encounter them.

In general, discernment always involves the evaluation of some kind of evidence. We can only accomplish this by using our five bodily senses: sight, hearing, smell, taste, or touch. We notice something; then we start sifting quickly through the incoming data. We discriminate between the pieces of evidence and detect patterns. Then we decide what to do, based in large part on what our discernment tells us.

Discerning (or distinguishing) of spirits is one of the gifts of the Holy Spirit (1 Cor. 12:10). This gift is a little different from the gift of the word of knowledge, in which facts are simply dropped into our minds or hearts. With discernment, you have to consider what is happening around you. Did what just happened make your skin prickle? Did the room just get brighter or darker? Did you hear a noise? Did you perhaps smell or taste something? Is what happened from a good source—or a bad one?

To discern spiritual realities, we need spiritual perception. We need to know what we're dealing with. Is this thing just my imagination, or is it coming from someone else's human spirit? Is it demonic? Is it in fact an angel? Is it the Holy Spirit?

God doesn't just take the gift of discerning of spirits and plug it into you, fully developed. Normally, it takes a lot of practice to get good at it, and some of your "discernment lessons" will involve making mistakes. That's also true of the learning process for your general discernment, which is part of your maturation as a disciple and which stems from Bible study, experience, and discipline. You will need both kinds of discernment when you find yourself involved with supernatural happenings. It's important for each of us to want to be one of "the mature, who because of practice have their senses trained to discern good and evil" (Heb. 5:14). Don't forget—you can always ask God to give you more ability to discern spirits and more mature discernment in general.

Angels Dancing in the Skies

Catherine Brown lives in Scotland and is the founder of a ministry called Gatekeepers Prayer and Mission. She tells about taking some young people with her to minister at a meeting and seeing angels afterward. It would seem that discernment should have been easy in this case, but at least one of the party found the experience hard to believe.

> The Lord sent angels to minister when I ministered with a group of young people in a small village in the central belt of Scotland.
>
> We had been praying and fasting and believing Jesus was going to save many at the meeting. Despite our faith and fasting, we did not see anyone commit their lives to Christ during the meeting, although the message was well received and the people delightful. The congregation were elderly, and at one point one dear old man fell down in the power of the Spirit. Not accustomed to seeing God working in this way, the people panicked and called an ambulance.

However, the elderly gentleman stood to his feet and said, "I'm fine. God was just dealing wi' me as the wee wifey [me!] was preaching." The ambulance was canceled, and the elderly congregation marveled at their God.

As we left the meeting, we began to thank Jesus in prayer that although we did not see with our eyes, we believed with our hearts that He was saving people in the village. Almost instantaneously, an angel appeared in the sky and was soon joined by another and another and another until the whole skyline was full of angelic beings swooping and looping and dancing. I literally parked the car right where we had stopped, and we all piled out into the highway in wonderment of what the Lord was allowing us to witness. There was tremendous power and glory being released, and we could hardly stand up under the weight of God's presence.

One young friend said with joy, "The Lord is saving people, because the angels celebrate when one sinner is being saved," and he was right. The angels were having a party, and we joined with them in celebration. What a privilege.

Eventually we got back into the car to head home. We had a two-hour drive ahead of us, and it was late at night. Soon one of the young women began to wander into unbelief and expressed this in her words that maybe we had just imagined what we had seen. Truth is, we had each seen the angels (ALL five of us), and in His gracious mercy the Lord allowed those angels to travel with us all the way home. The unbelief fell off our young friend as faith covered her tender heart. It was only when we neared our hometowns that the angels took off on another glory mission.

Thankfully my precious husband was still awake as we burst in the door, our faces glowing with joy and our mouths full of loud testimonies to God's saving grace!

Catherine and her young friends saw those angels with their eyes, to their delighted astonishment. They also felt God's power in the atmosphere. Even so, the one girl doubted for a while what she had seen. But when she continued to see them, she realized it couldn't be her imagination, and she returned to her original discernment about the matter.

The purpose of the angels' appearance was obvious—it was to encourage them in their work, to build their faith, and to communicate heaven's joy at the hidden results of their mission.

Discerning the angelic presence isn't something we think about between supernatural happenings. Surely those young people didn't expect to see angels in the sky after their little mission. But such happenings usually occur when we least expect them, so it's best to keep our "discerners" in good working order.

Testing the Spirits

On the morning Jesus rose from the dead, Mary Magdalene went weeping to the tomb, where she encountered two angels dressed in white. She had already been there earlier and had noticed that the grave-sealing stone had been moved away. She had run to fetch Peter and John, and they had marveled to see the empty tomb and the cast-off graveclothes. (See John 20:1–20.)

The men had left to go to their homes, but she had lingered at the tomb, grieving what she thought was now a double loss—first His death and now His stolen body. Suddenly she saw one angel sitting at the head of the empty place where Jesus's body had been and another sitting at the foot.

But wait—how did she know they were angels? Was it simply that what she saw defied any other explanation? I don't think the angels said to her, "Hello, Mary. We are two angels." Instead, their first words to her were, "Woman, why are you weeping?" (John 20:13).

Immediately, she turned and saw someone she thought was the gardener, but He turned out to be her beloved Jesus, fully *alive*, no longer dead (and certainly not stolen). The angels had come to help her understand. After all, with her own eyes she had seen Him lifeless just the day before. She needed angelic help, especially because of her blinding grief, to comprehend the glorious fact that He had risen from the grave. These were truly angels, not a creation of her overwrought brain or, worse, evil imposters. Jesus had truly risen from the grave, alive.

That day, the disciple John may have missed the angels because he left before they appeared, but over the course of his long life he saw plenty of angels—both light and dark ones. He's the one who wrote in his Gospel about the angels Mary saw, and he's also the one who included the following advice in one of his letters to the young church:

> Beloved, do not believe every spirit, but test the spirits to see whether they are from God, because many false prophets have gone out into the world. By this you know the Spirit of God: every spirit that confesses that Jesus Christ has come in the flesh is from God; and every spirit that does not confess Jesus is not from God; this is the spirit of the antichrist, of which you have heard that it is coming, and now it is already in the world.
>
> —1 John 4:1–3

In another letter to the young church, the apostle Paul added that we must "prove all things; hold fast that which is good" (1 Thess. 5:21, KJV). The message here is that we need to *test the spirits*. We absolutely need to do this, lest we be deceived and misled by the evil one. After all, he does masquerade as an "angel of light" (2 Cor. 11:14). In other words, his counterfeits of heavenly things can look and sound pretty authentic. Remember how Pharaoh's court magicians were able to replicate several of the plagues God sent? (See Exodus 7–8.)

Not only does satan masquerade as an angel in good standing, but he also finds it relatively easy to prey on the weaknesses of human beings. Actually, the human heart doesn't need very much enemy input to produce its own misguided notions: "The heart is deceitful above all things, and desperately wicked" (Jer. 17:9, KJV). Besides satan, his demons, and false prophets, we have to contend with true believers who have true encounters with God—only to add their own human insights and interpretations. We need to be able to discern the spirit behind each message!

Seducing and Familiar Spirits

For example, we need to be familiar with familiar spirits—and I don't mean familiar as in "friendly"! We need to be aware of their existence and their tactics.

Seducing or deceiving demonic spirits are evil emissaries from the dark side. They come to entice, lure, attract, arouse, or fascinate somebody in order to bring the person into captivity. They are like demonic forerunners, paving the way for other dark spirits who can do even more damage. Deceptive, seducing spirits sear a person's conscience, "as with a hot iron":

> The [Holy] Spirit distinctly and expressly declares that in latter times some will turn away from the faith, giving attention to deluding and seducing spirits and doctrines that demons teach, through the hypocrisy and pretensions of liars whose consciences are seared (cauterized).
>
> —1 Timothy 4:1–2, AMP

The term "familiar spirit" is used to describe a specific kind of seducing spirit, one that takes on the form of a physical body often familiar to the individual being deceived. The term is used in the King James Version in Deuteronomy 18:9–12, in 1 Samuel 28:3, 7–8, and Leviticus 19:31, and it refers to a false apparition that brings a purported message from God. The Book of Leviticus warns, "Regard not them that have familiar spirits, neither seek after wizards, to be defiled by them: I am the LORD your God" (Lev. 19:31, KJV). These entities may appear in one form in one generation and adapt to another form in another generation, always with the same ultimate purpose: to deceive and capture unsuspecting people.

Because these spirits are adaptive, it is difficult to discern them without the help of the Holy Spirit. Be alert to shape-shifting spirits, especially those who impersonate a deceased loved one or a biblical figure, or who attempt to appear as a true angelic messenger.

Nine Scriptural Tests

Anytime you need to discern spiritual activity, you should apply the following biblical tests to it. (This remains true even for highly gifted, mature saints.)

1. Edification, consolation, exhortation. Does the spiritual event build up the people of God? Even when Jeremiah delivered a negative word, his message contained an upbuilding promise from God for those who were obedient. (See Jeremiah 1:10ff.) First Corinthians 14 contains these pieces of advice: "He who prophesies speaks edification and exhortation and comfort to men" and "Let all things be done for edification" (1 Cor. 14:3, 26, NKJV). In Catherine Brown's account above, the angels brought joy and delight to the group in the car, building their faith and giving them encouragement about the success of their mission.

2. Agreement with the Bible. Is there scriptural support for what happened? "All Scripture is inspired by God" (2 Tim. 3:16). Authentic spiritual experiences line up with the message of biblical accounts, prophecies, and teaching. We can apply this test to the account above also, in which one of the young people thought of Jesus's words in Luke 15:10 (NKJV): "There is joy in the presence of the angels of God over one sinner who repents." (Besides, we all know the Gospel account of the sky being full of angels the night Jesus was born in Bethlehem.)

3. Exaltation of Jesus. True spiritual experiences glorify Jesus Christ first and foremost, not a person or an angel or a manifestation. Sometimes we need course correction, though. John did: "And I fell at his feet to worship him [the angel]. But he said to me, 'See that you do not do that! I am your fellow servant, and of your brethren who have the testimony of Jesus. Worship God! For the testimony of Jesus is the spirit of prophecy'" (Rev. 19:10, NKJV).

4. Good fruit. Has the spiritual encounter borne good fruit of the Holy Spirit? (See Ephesians 5:9 and Galatians 5:22–23.) Or has it stirred up prideful arrogance, boastfulness, exaggeration, dishonesty, covetousness, licentiousness, immorality, addictions, financial irresponsibility, broken marriage vows, weakened churches, or broken homes? Even a single one of those "warning fruits" is enough to flag an experience as suspect. "'Beware of false prophets, who come to you in sheep's clothing, but inwardly they are ravenous wolves. You will know them by their fruits. Do men gather grapes from thornbushes or figs from thistles? Even so, every good tree bears good fruit, but a bad tree bears bad fruit'" (Matt. 7:15–17, NKJV).

5. Accurate predictions. If the spiritual experience involved a prophetic prediction of the future, did the prediction come true? The Bible tells us:

> You may say to yourselves, "How can we know when a message has *not* been spoken by the LORD?" If what a prophet proclaims in the name of the LORD does *not* take place or come true, that is a message the LORD has *not* spoken. That prophet has spoken presumptuously. Do not be afraid of him.
>
> —Deuteronomy 18:21–22, NIV, emphasis added

Now, this isn't just a straight true-or-false test. A prediction can be a mixture of true revelation and human or demonic ideas. A conditional prediction, such as the one Jonah gave to Nineveh, may never come to pass. (Nineveh repented, so God did not destroy the city.) There are also cases in which the timeline involved, such as the Old Testament predictions about the Messiah's coming, is too long to bear scrutiny by one generation.

6. Accurate predictions must turn people toward God. It's not enough to be correct. A spiritual experience that gives an accurate glimpse into the future must also affect people positively, turning them toward God.

> If a prophet, or one who foretells by dreams, appears among you and announces to you a miraculous sign or wonder, and if the sign or wonder of which he has spoken takes place, and he says, "Let us follow other gods" (gods you have not known) "and let us worship them," you must not listen to the words of that prophet or dreamer. The LORD your God is testing you to find out whether you love him

with all your heart and with all your soul. It is the LORD your God you must follow, and him you must revere. Keep his commands and obey him; serve him and hold fast to him.

—Deuteronomy 13:1–4, NIV

7. Liberty or bondage? Does the overall effect of the experience produce greater liberty in people—or increased bondage? The Holy Spirit never enslaves or manipulates us. He does not motivate us by fear or legalism: "For you did not receive the spirit of bondage again to fear, but you received the Spirit of adoption by whom we cry out, 'Abba, Father'" (Rom. 8:15, NKJV). "For God hath not given us the spirit of fear; but of power, and of love, and of a sound mind" (2 Tim. 1:7, KJV).

8. Life giving or death dealing? This is similar to the test just above. Was the spiritual event life giving, or did it serve to crush joy and hope and health? Jesus said, "I am...the life" (John 14:6). It is the Spirit of Jesus "Who has qualified us [making us to be fit and worthy and sufficient] as ministers and dispensers of a new covenant [of salvation through Christ], not [ministers] of the letter (of legally written code) but of the Spirit; for the code [of the Law] kills, but *the [Holy] Spirit makes alive*" (2 Cor. 3:6, AMP, emphasis added).

9. Witness of truth. Does the Holy Spirit bear witness to your spirit that the experience and its message are true? This is quite subjective, so this test *must* be applied in conjunction with the other tests above. And yet, the Holy Spirit within a believer should always bear witness or confirm a true visitation or spiritual experience. After all, the Holy Spirit is "the Spirit of truth" (John 16:13).

As for you, the anointing you received from him remains in you, and you do not need anyone to teach you. But as his anointing teaches you about all things and as that anointing is real, not counterfeit— just as it has taught you, remain in him.

—1 John 2:27, NIV

Discerning Spirits With Your Five Senses

At the beginning of this chapter, I made the point that the only "discerning equipment" we possess, in addition to our Holy Spirit–anointed human spirits (which can sometimes be called our "sixth sense"), consists of our five bodily senses: sight, hearing, smell, taste, or touch. None of us end up using all of our senses to the same degree. We tend to "specialize" because of our God-given personalities and types of experiences. At the same time we need to remember that if we find ourselves in the midst of an unusual spiritual experience, it might be one of our less-used senses that can best contribute to our discernment.

For example, for many people, *sight* is the biggie. What if, one day, one of these vision-oriented people begins to *smell* something. That's it, just a smell. Nothing else is happening. It's not a good smell; it's the acrid smell of ammonia. "Ah, a *bad* smell!" he thinks. "So therefore a bad spirit must be in the room." He scrutinizes the place, but his eyes tell him nothing. He does notice that he doesn't feel bad. On the contrary, he feels fine, merely curious, somewhat "prophetic."

When he started to smell it, he happened to be interceding for his church. He's *in* the church, as a matter of fact. But he's quite sure that nothing in the vicinity (wooden pews, old carpet on the floor, hymnbooks, and Bibles) could be carrying this unmistakable smell. "It reminds me of when I was a kid in school, after lunch, when the lunch workers would wash the lunchroom tables down with ammonia and water....Ammonia is a cleansing agent. God, what are You telling me here?"

In all likelihood, there is no sulfur-breathing evil spirit in the room at all. Almost for sure no human janitor had just come through with an ammonia-soaked rag. But probably an angel did just come through, carrying the message from God: "I am going to cleanse this church." As the intercessor figures this out, he can pray according to God's will, and he can expect to see this prophetic sense fulfilled. It really takes discernment to know what to do.

Basically, discernment is perception. Sometimes it is as simple as an inner knowledge, a "gut feeling" that we cannot explain. That kind of spiritual perception is often so subtle that we can easily miss it or dismiss it as a mere hunch. But the more we yield our natural senses to the Lord, the more God can anoint them and make them more sensitive to discern. It's a progressive unfolding.

I saw...

You see things with your two eyes wide open. You also can see things with your eyes closed, you know—visions are often seen this way. You also see things when you're sleeping—unless you are physically blind, almost 100 percent of your dreams will be memorable because of their visual content. When you're doing most of your dreaming, your eyes are darting back and forth behind your closed eyelids (REM sleep, or rapid eye movement).

It's no wonder that, with so many ways of *seeing*, we so often rely on our sense of sight when we're discerning supernatural events. Our sight—both external and internal—is one of our most valuable senses. Sometimes it may be no more than a flash of light that brings a strong sense of a spiritual presence into the room. Other times, we may see an outline form or even a kind of fog of God's glory filling a room. We may observe a kind of shimmering presence or, of course, a fully defined vision, perceived in our mind's eye or with our wide-open physical eyes.

The prophet Ezekiel was overwhelmed with visual input. "In the thirtieth year, in the fourth month on the fifth day, while I was among the exiles by the Kebar River, the heavens were opened and I saw visions of God" (Ezek. 1:1, NIV). He goes on to describe in detail what he saw in heaven: a fiery windstorm; four living creatures with four faces each, four wings, and four hands; four wheels full of eyes; and much, much more. (See Ezekiel 1–3.)

In Catherine Brown's account related earlier in this chapter, she and the young people saw those angels with their physical eyes. They had their eyes wide open, and the angels stayed within view for a long time. Apparently, John the beloved disciple saw with his physical eyes what he received from the angel in his Book of Revelation, although, interestingly, he first heard a voice like a trumpet, and...

> Then I turned to *see* the voice that was speaking with me. And having turned I *saw* seven golden lampstands; and in the middle of the lampstands I *saw* one like a son of man, clothed in a robe reaching to the feet, and girded across His chest with a golden sash. His head and His hair were white like white wool, like snow; and His eyes were like a flame of fire.
>
> —Revelation 1:12–14, emphasis added

In other words, John quite naturally *looked* with his eyes to see what had made the loud sound. And there was plenty to see, including a number of angels:

> I saw another strong angel coming down out of heaven, clothed with a cloud; and the rainbow was upon his head, and his face was like the sun, and his feet like pillars of fire; and he had in his hand a little book which was open. He placed his right foot on the sea and his left on the land.
>
> —Revelation 10:1–2

In providing you with scriptural examples of the different kinds of sight that we can use in discerning the angelic presence, I don't want to omit visual dreams. Here's the description of Joseph's dream regarding his all-important decision to wed Mary:

> And Joseph her husband, being a righteous man and not wanting to disgrace her, planned to send her away secretly. But when he had considered this, behold, an angel of the Lord appeared to him in a dream, saying, "Joseph, son of David, do not be afraid to take Mary as your wife; for the Child who has been conceived in her is of the Holy Spirit."
>
> —Matthew 1:19–20

Joseph first saw the angel, and then he heard the angel's voice. Seeing and hearing are often intertwined, aren't they? Let's look at some scriptural examples of how people discern spirits through *hearing*.

I heard...

When Joseph saw the angel in his dream, the angel spoke directly to him.

Later in the New Testament, we read about Cornelius, who "clearly saw in a vision an angel of God." Cornelius hadn't expected *that*. He was jolted even more when the angel spoke his name in a commanding voice, "Cornelius!"

> And he [the angel] said to him, "Your prayers and alms have ascended as a memorial before God. Now dispatch some men to Joppa and send for a man named Simon, who is also called Peter; he is staying with a tanner named Simon, whose house is by the sea."
> —Acts 10:3–6

Those were pretty specific directions. Cornelius didn't waste any time. He gathered his men and dispatched them to Joppa. No one had to teach him about discerning what he had heard. He knew he had received a message from God.

Even though hearing is one of the most common ways of receiving a heavenly message, it's not limited to hearing spoken words or sentences. People can hear the sound of wind, such as occurred on the Day of Pentecost. That happened to Michal Ann and me that time when a supernatural wind came blowing through our closed bedroom window and woke us up to receive angelic visitors.

People hear bells, thunder, a telephone ringing, or heavenly music. The variety of options is endless. I know a woman who was awakened from sleep by a small noise, only to overhear a short conversation between two angels, whose illuminated faces she could just make out as they stood next to her bed. "Is she really going to do it?" said one, referring to a very difficult undertaking that the woman was feeling led to initiate the next day. "Yes," said the other. That's all she saw or heard, but that snatch of conversation assured her that she could expect angelic help in the morning.

Her experience was a little less dramatic (but no less welcome) than what happened to Paul in the middle of the great storm at sea. As he reported it to the others who were on the storm-tossed vessel:

> Yet now I urge you to keep up your courage, for there will be no loss of life among you, but only of the ship. For this very night an angel of the God to whom I belong and whom I serve stood before me, saying, "Do not be afraid, Paul; you must stand before Caesar; and behold, God has granted you all those who are sailing with you."
>
> —Acts 27:22–24

Keep looking, keep listening, and keep tuning in with all of your other senses to distinguish God's envoys from counterfeit messengers.

I smelled...

As noted in the example earlier in this chapter, spiritual discernment can sometimes come through our sense of smell. Many people have testified to sensing the presence of the Lord accompanied by the smell of roses.

At times, it is possible to identify the enemy's presence in the same way. A particular place just may not "smell right," even if we don't quite know why. Sometimes we can identify a rotten-egg odor or other noxious smell. If there is no logical, natural explanation for the unpleasant odor, it may be an indicator that an unclean spirit is present.

I have found that I am able to discern a certain form of addiction in a person's life by using my sense of smell. I can smell a type of smoke that I associate with the addiction, and then I know how to proceed in ministering to the person involved.

The sense of smell is not prominently portrayed in the Bible accounts of discernment, in spite of the fact that we ourselves, indwelt by the Holy Spirit, are described as carrying His "sweet savour" to the world around us:

But thanks be to God, Who in Christ always leads us in triumph [as trophies of Christ's victory] and through us spreads and makes evident the fragrance of the knowledge of God everywhere, for we are the sweet fragrance of Christ [which exhales] unto God, [discernible alike] among those who are being saved and among those who are perishing.

—2 Corinthians 2:14–15, AMP

I tasted...

What about discerning a spiritual presence through the sense of taste? Have you ever heard someone say, "That just leaves a bad taste in my mouth"?

The prophet Ezekiel (whose extensive experiences could be used to illustrate all five senses in overdrive) was treated to a spiritual tasting incident. Remember the scroll he was told to eat?

"And you, son of man, do not be afraid of them or their words. Do not be afraid, though briers and thorns are all around you and you live among scorpions. Do not be afraid of what they say or terrified by them, though they are a rebellious house. You must speak my words to them, whether they listen or fail to listen, for they are rebellious. But you, son of man, listen to what I say to you. Do not rebel like that rebellious house; open your mouth and eat what I give you."

Then I looked, and I saw a hand stretched out to me. In it was a scroll, which he unrolled before me. On both sides of it were written words of lament and mourning and woe.

And he said to me, "Son of man, eat what is before you, eat this scroll; then go and speak to the house of Israel." So I opened my mouth, and he gave me the scroll to eat. Then he said to me, "Son of man, eat this scroll I am giving you and fill your stomach with it." So I ate it, and it tasted as sweet as honey in my mouth.

—Ezekiel 2:6–3:3, NIV

Another supernatural scroll was consumed by John, who recorded what it tasted like:

So I went to the angel and asked him to give me the little scroll. He said to me, "Take it and eat it. It will turn your stomach sour [bitter], but in your mouth it will be as sweet as honey." I took the little scroll from the angel's hand and ate it. It tasted as sweet as honey in my mouth, but when I had eaten it, my stomach turned sour.

—Revelation 10:9–10, NIV

I felt...

I don't want anybody to be confused when I start talking about getting discernment through *feeling*. It's certainly true that we can feel or "sense" spirits, but here I want to refer strictly to physical touch, the kind of feeling that happens through the nerves in your skin. And, yes, angels do touch people to get their attention, to communicate with them, and sometimes to hurt them, if they're bringing God's judgment. Here are a few scriptural examples, with the "touch words" in italics:

Then the angel who was speaking with me returned and *roused* me, as a man who is awakened from his sleep.

—Zechariah 4:1

And at once an angel of the Lord *smote* him and *cut him down*, because he did not give God the glory (the preeminence and kingly majesty that belong to Him as the supreme Ruler); and he was eaten by worms and died.

—Acts 12:23, AMP

Suddenly an angel of the Lord appeared and a light shone in the cell. He *struck* Peter on the side and woke him up. "Quick, get up!" he said, and the chains fell off Peter's wrists.

—Acts 12:7, NIV

Your sense of touch comes into play when your skin or scalp tingles, and also when you feel pain that is meant to communicate a message to you. At times I receive physical pains in my heart that indicate to me that some kind of heart wound has occurred in another person's life.

These pains alert me to be ready to minister freedom and healing to the other person.

So we see that we can discern spirits (angelic, human, and demonic) by various means if we are anointed with the Spirit of God. At different times, people *see, hear, smell, taste,* or *feel* the touch of another spirit. Our Holy Spirit–filled spirits are our ultimate sensors, and we can continue to grow and mature in this realm for as long as we live here on Earth.

> *Holy Spirit, we present to You our eyes (our natural eyes and the eyes of our hearts), and we ask You to anoint them to perceive, to distinguish, and to differentiate. We present all of our senses to You, and we ask You to keep us on track. Anoint our senses to perceive heavenly realities. Help us to steer clear of counterfeit spiritual experiences. May complete access be given to the Word of the Lord in our lives. We are covered with Jesus's blood. Amen.*

Prayer is the soul's sincere desire,
Unuttered or expressed,
The motion of a bidden fire
That trembles in the breast.
Prayer is the burden of a sigh,
The falling of a tear,
The upward glancing of an eye,
When none but God is near.
Prayer is the contrite sinner's voice,
Returning from his ways,
While angels in their songs rejoice
And cry, "Behold, he prays!"[1]

T E N

Angelic Intervention Through Intercession

When God hears prayers from His people, He responds. What happens is that He dispatches His angels before, during, and after our prayers. It's a dynamic, living sequence, repeated over and over:

- Angels usher in God's presence and declare His intentions to people.

- As a result, Spirit-inspired intercession rises from believers.

- In response to the prayers, God releases His angels to deliver, protect, heal, and strengthen people; to execute His judgments; to reap and to gather; and to do whatever else He wants them to do.

Do you think about this when you pray? That prayer you prayed this morning may be the one that God used to mobilize an army of angels. This means your intercessory prayers are important! It also means that it may have been *angels* who helped you know what to pray before the word was on your lips. Angels can come to prepare the way for your prayers, to convey your prayers to heaven, and to execute the answers to those prayers.

Reviewing the Basics

Let's quickly run through some important facts that are foundational to this chapter. I want to consolidate what you already know by posing these questions: What is intercession? How are angels' assignments related to our intercession?

What is intercession?

Somebody who intercedes intervenes in a situation, stepping between two parties with the intention of reconciling differences. An intercessor is a "go-between." An intercessor mediates, occupying a middle position. The most familiar phrase is "standing in the gap," which comes from Ezekiel 22:30 (God speaking): "I sought for a man among them, that should make up the hedge, and stand in the gap before me for the land, that I should not destroy it: but I found none" (kjv).

In my book *The Prophetic Intercessor,* I defined intercession as follows: "The act of making a request to a superior, or expressing a deep-seated yearning to our one and only superior, God." I followed that with a definition of intercessor: "One who reminds God of His promises and appointments yet to be fulfilled; who takes up a case of injustice before God on behalf of another; who makes up the 'hedge' (that is, builds up the wall in time of battle); and who stands in the gap between God's righteous judgments and the people's need for mercy."[2]

Jesus, our High Priest, who sacrificed His own life to redeem us from death, is the foremost intercessor. He interposed Himself between sinful humans and the justified wrath of His Father, and He still intercedes for us, day and night. We read in the Book of Hebrews, "Therefore He is able also to save forever those who draw near to God through Him, since He always lives to make intercession for them" (Heb. 7:25).

All believers are called to be intercessors. We co-labor with Jesus Christ. We lift up to our Father every need, every desire, and every thought. The Bible is filled with urgent summons to pray: "Rejoice always; *pray without ceasing*; in everything give thanks; for this is God's will for you in Christ Jesus" (1 Thess. 5:16–18, emphasis added).

How are angels' assignments related to our intercession?

We don't hear as much about the relationship of angels to our intercession as we do about the intercession itself. I want to take the three points above and relate them to some of the specific angelic assignments that we learned about in the sixth chapter.

1. Angels usher in God's presence and declare His intentions to people. By definition, angels are assigned *to minister the presence of the Lord*. They usher in His glory. They connect heaven and the earth. Sometimes we feel God's glory, and usually we don't, but they never stop ushering it in.

Another one of their stated functions is *to be messengers pronouncing God's will*, although they're not always as dramatic as they were in the skies over Bethlehem when Jesus was born:

> In the same region there were some shepherds staying out in the fields and keeping watch over their flock by night. And an angel of the Lord suddenly stood before them, and the glory of the Lord shone around them; and they were terribly frightened. But the angel said to them, "Do not be afraid; for behold, I bring you good news of great joy which will be for all the people; for today in the city of David there has been born for you a Savior, who is Christ the Lord."
>
> —Luke 2:8–11

Angels may simply pronounce God's will in the silence of your prayer time, dropping into your mind and heart the very thing that God wants to do—and that your inspired prayers can subsequently bring about. Angels sometimes *release wisdom and understanding in dreams or visions*. In a variety of ways, angels *help to give guidance and direction* to human beings, who are their fellow servants, earthbound, and in need of heavenly assistance.

2. As a result of having been ushered into God's presence and learning His will, intercession rises from believers. Angels are involved in our responses to God's guidance. They are involved in our *praise and worship*. They come from the throne room, after all, where worship ascends perpetually. Angels worship with us, and they enhance our praises. Without their help to cultivate grateful, expectant, worshipful hearts, we cannot carry out our function as intercessors. Paul wrote to the Philippians, "Do not be anxious about anything, but in everything, by prayer and petition, *with thanksgiving*, present your requests to God" (Phil. 4:6, NIV, emphasis added).

Angels are *divine watchers*. They look into the historical affairs of humans. They mentor us in alert and prayerful watching. They tip us off when they see something. (See Daniel 4:13–17; Acts 12:20–23; 1 Timothy 5:21.) They also tip each other off, and they go to battle whenever the need arises. Angels are definitely involved in our *spiritual warfare*. We can't stand against the devil without them.

3. In response to our prayers, God releases His angels. They bring the answers to our prayers. They carry God's provision from His storeroom.

The angels bring *deliverance*, and they *bind demonic powers*. They provide *protection* and *strength* to people. God uses them as His *healing* instruments. They *execute His judgments*. They are His *reapers and gatherers*. They stand ready to do whatever He wants them to do.

Five Foundational Premises

Another way of talking about it is to identify five foundational premises that underline the truth that angels are intimately involved with our intercession. They are as follows: (1) believers are co-workers with Christ; (2) God hears and answers prayers; (3) an innumerable company of angels is available; (4) angels are involved in both the spiritual and practical affairs of humankind; and (5) angels deliver God's answers to people's prayers.

1. Believers are co-workers with Christ. Here is a phrase for you to remember: *God's resources are released by man's invitation of intercession.* We do not have a passive role to play. We are actively inviting God to get involved in human affairs, both small and sweeping. "The effectual fervent prayer of a righteous man availeth much" (James 5:16, KJV).

2. God hears and answers prayers. This is very basic; we absolutely *must* operate on this premise. God does not turn a deaf ear to our prayers. In fact, our prayerful intercession influences Him to advance direction and destinies of individuals and entire nations.

3. An innumerable company of angels is available. Heaven's army of the angelic host is waiting for its next assignment. Each angel is ready to be dispatched. Angels, in a manner of speaking, are unemployed—at least between assignments. They are waiting for our invitation in order to be released to most of their assignments.

Nobody can count them, there are so many: "The host of heaven cannot be counted and the sand of the sea cannot be measured" (Jer. 33:22).

4. Angels are involved in both the spiritual and practical affairs of humankind. Sometimes we think that angels are only involved in the hyper-spiritual stuff such as the Bethlehems, or at least protection from imminent danger. We are under the impression that angelic assistance happens only once in a while. I don't think so. I *know* angels have preserved me from traffic accidents time and time again. (Somebody once told me, "James, you must have more squashed angels than anybody.")

Angels are servants, and they do practical tasks. Remember the story of Peter and the angel who came into his jail cell to let him go free? "He [the angel] woke him up....Then the angel said to him, 'Put on your clothes and sandals.' And Peter did so. 'Wrap your cloak around you and follow me,' the angel told him" (Acts 12:7–8, NIV). That's a *practical* assignment!

5. Angels deliver God's answers to people's prayers. I don't think we can differentiate between God's direct answers to our prayers and His "indirect" answers, conveyed by angels. The angels are often His best option, and they *are* direct. They're obedient; they're fast; they're powerfully efficient. They carry God's love and His character. What more could you want?

The important thing is that God answers prayers. The "extra credit" part is recognizing that angels have an important role in delivering His answers.

Scriptural Examples of Angelic Intervention Through Intercession

The classic biblical example of how human intervention can affect divine initiatives is the story of Abraham's negotiations regarding the fate of the cities of Sodom and Gomorrah. Abraham had just finished talking with his three angelic visitors. They departed, and then God decided to make known to Abraham how He viewed the evil population of the cities of Sodom and Gomorrah:

> And the LORD said, "The outcry of Sodom and Gomorrah is indeed great, and their sin is exceedingly grave. I will go down now, and see if they have done entirely according to its outcry, which has come to Me; and if not, I will know."...
>
> Abraham came near and said, "Will You indeed sweep away the righteous with the wicked? Suppose there are fifty righteous within the city; will You indeed sweep it away and not spare the place for the sake of the fifty righteous who are in it? Far be it from You to do such a thing, to slay the righteous with the wicked, so that the righteous and the wicked are treated alike. Far be it from You! Shall not the Judge of all the earth deal justly?"
>
> So the LORD said, "If I find in Sodom fifty righteous within the city, then I will spare the whole place on their account."
>
> And Abraham replied, "Now behold, I have ventured to speak to the Lord, although I am but dust and ashes."
>
> —Genesis 18:20–21, 23–27

You know how the story goes. Abraham kept bargaining God down, always humble and yet with incredible confidence that God is both merciful and just. He counted down by fives until he got to thirty, and God kept agreeing not to destroy the city if He found that many righteous men inside.

Then suddenly Abraham started jumping downward by tens, until he got down to a mere ten righteous people. God's response was, "'I will not destroy it on account of the ten'" (Gen. 18:32).

I don't know why Abraham stopped at ten. Maybe he hit the limit of his faith. But regardless of why he stopped, the principle is clear—God stops when we stop. It's like that with our prayers, too. God might even provoke us to pray longer by saying, "How much do you want?" He responds to the persistent, hungry cries of desperate men and women who are praying according to their faith and their sphere of authority.

Where Sodom and Gomorrah were concerned, ten righteous men could not be found, so God was going to carry out His threat. But first He sent two angels to protect and deliver Abraham's nephew Lot and his family.

> Now the two angels came to Sodom in the evening as Lot was sitting in the gate of Sodom. When Lot saw them, he rose to meet them and bowed down with his face to the ground. And he said, "Now behold, my lords, please turn aside into your servant's house, and spend the night, and wash your feet; then you may rise early and go on your way."
>
> They said however, "No, but we shall spend the night in the square."
>
> Yet he urged them strongly, so they turned aside to him and entered his house; and he prepared a feast for them, and baked unleavened bread, and they ate.
>
> —Genesis 19:1–3

Lot, a mere man, related directly to the angels, and he dissuaded them, evidently with some effort, from spending the night in the public square. They came home with him, and they even ate the food he prepared for them.

Then, suddenly, things got ugly. The men of Sodom, living up to—or *down* to—their evil reputation, pounded on the door to demand to have sexual relations with Lot's guests! They were predatory and rapacious. In desperation, Lot offered them his own virgin daughters instead. But they wouldn't listen. In fact, it appeared that they were going to kill Lot by stampeding him against his own front door.

At the last minute, the angels somehow snatched Lot into the house and shut the door securely against the mob. To top it off, they struck every last one of the marauding men with blindness so that all they could do was grope unsuccessfully, trying to find the door.

The next day, "the angels urged Lot, saying, 'Up, take your wife and your two daughters who are here, or you will be swept away in the punishment of the city.' But he hesitated. So the men seized his hand and the hand of his wife and the hands of his two daughters, for the compassion of the LORD was upon him; and they brought him out, and put him outside the city" (Gen. 19:15–16). These are "hands-on" angels! And they seem to have a clear idea of God's heart and God's intentions.

Even now, Lot tries to negotiate some more. He spies a nearby town, and he asks the angels to let him find refuge there. Perhaps originally it had been slated for destruction with Sodom and Gomorrah, but the angels, speaking with God's full authority, agree not to destroy little Zoar. This was a detour from God's best purposes for Lot and his family, but God respected Lot's free will and allowed him to flee to Zoar. Apparently the angel of the Lord must operate within the limits of Lot's willingness, because he said, "Hurry, escape there, for I cannot do anything until you arrive there" (v. 22). They arrived, and fire and brimstone destroyed the evil cities.

The destruction isn't really the most important feature of the story. What's amazing is the way that both Abraham and Lot related to God and His angels. God remembered Abraham's intercession, to the point that the angels were not released to destroy the cities until the safety of Lot's family had been secured, against considerable obstacles. Abraham had taken a stand between the dead and the living, and God sent angels of protection for the sake of the four who needed to be saved.

I wonder what would have happened if Abraham had bartered down to four. Perhaps the other parts of this disaster (the vicious mob attack, the pillar of salt) would not have occurred. Abraham and Lot never found out, and we'll never know for sure either. It underlines the main point for everyone who has ever heard this story: "Don't quit! Heaven's resources are released in response to man's invitation. Don't ever quit!"

Daniel, Peter, and Angels

Two other familiar stories from the Bible provide further examples of the power of intercession and the involvement of angels in response to prayer.

We know that Daniel prayed—a lot. He got in trouble for it more than once, but that didn't stop him. After many ups and downs in Babylon, to which he had been exiled as a young man, Daniel, having earned favor and authority, set himself to intercede for his people. He wrote, "So I gave my attention to the Lord God to seek Him by prayer and supplications, with fasting, sackcloth and ashes" (Dan. 9:3).

He prayed and confessed generational sins of Israel, "standing in the gap" so completely that he could identify with and repent for sins that he himself had not committed. He prayed desperately for three weeks, with no sign of a breakthrough, beseeching God to act on behalf of His chosen people: "O Lord, hear! O Lord, forgive! O Lord, listen and take action! For Your own sake, O my God, do not delay, because Your city and Your people are called by Your name" (v. 19).

Then, finally, something happened. The archangel Gabriel himself came to Daniel:

> Now while I was speaking and praying, and confessing my sin and the sin of my people Israel, and presenting my supplication before the LORD my God in behalf of the holy mountain of my God, while I was still speaking in prayer, then the man Gabriel, whom I had seen in the vision previously, came to me in my extreme weariness about the time of the evening offering.
>
> He gave me instruction and talked with me and said, "O Daniel, I have now come forth to give you insight with understanding. At

the beginning of your supplications the command was issued, and I have come to tell you, for you are highly esteemed; so give heed to the message and gain understanding of the vision."

—Daniel 9:20–23

Do you see what happened here? Gabriel came *in response to Daniel's words*. He goes on to explain how his coming was impeded by the prince of Persia (an evil principality), but that he actually responded right away, twenty-one days before, when Daniel first set himself to pray. Quite likely he and the archangel Michael could not have continued to press through the well-entrenched opposition if Daniel had not continued to pray and humble himself.

The connection is loud and clear—our persistent, informed intercession releases angelic action. We have the authority to "pray in" the reinforcements that we need. We can and should call forth angelic intervention by means of our prayerful invitations.

Peter's "prayed-in" angel

Hundreds of years after Daniel (remember—God and His angels don't change), along came Peter. His evangelistic activities had gotten him into hot water with the ruling authorities, and he was locked up in prison under the guard of four squads of soldiers. Herod had just had James killed. The church was under siege. However, the church was praying!

> And behold, an angel of the Lord suddenly appeared and a light shone in the cell; and he struck Peter's side and woke him up, saying, "Get up quickly." And his chains fell off his hands. And the angel said to him, "Gird yourself and put on your sandals." And he did so. And he said to him, "Wrap your cloak around you and follow me."
>
> And he went out and continued to follow, and he did not know that what was being done by the angel was real, but thought he was seeing a vision. When they had passed the first and second guard, they came to the iron gate that leads into the city, which opened

for them by itself; and they went out and went along one street, and immediately the angel departed from him.

When Peter came to himself, he said, "Now I know for sure that the Lord has sent forth His angel and rescued me from the hand of Herod and from all that the Jewish people were expecting." And when he realized this, he went to the house of Mary, the mother of John who was also called Mark, where many were gathered together and were praying.

When he knocked at the door of the gate, a servant-girl named Rhoda came to answer. When she recognized Peter's voice, because of her joy she did not open the gate, but ran in and announced that Peter was standing in front of the gate.

They said to her, "You are out of your mind!" But she kept insisting that it was so. They kept saying, "It is his angel."

But Peter continued knocking; and when they had opened the door, they saw him and were amazed.

—Acts 12:7–16

Don't you love this story? Would Peter have been delivered from prison (and likely death) if the church had not prayed fervently? I don't think so. Herod never had another chance to lay his hands on Peter.

In response to the united, passionate prayers of the saints, an angel came right into the prison, disregarding the guards and the gates and the bars, and set Peter free. Let's renew our own prayers today! God's angels are ready to respond, quickly and decisively. They are eager to be dispatched to warn, deliver, protect, guide, enable, and do warfare.

Prayer, Judgment, and Mercy

My friend Shawn Bolz had an experience that shows yet another type of angelic assignment, one that is sure to stimulate and release endless intercessory prayers heavenward. Here, in his words, is what he saw:

In a recent spiritual experience, I saw a key coming down from Heaven. It wasn't like any key I have ever seen before. It was living and breathing and it had light shining from it—it was an angelic being. I was in awe of what I was seeing, and I watched as the angel started to shoot through the earth, unlocking thousands of doors in one sweep. When the doors were unlocked, the key would go back into the heavens, and then dive back down opening up thousands of more doors.

The Lord asked me, "What are you seeing, Shawn?"

I said, "I see an angel that looks like a key opening doors."

The voice from Heaven was Jesus Himself, and He spoke, "This is My very angel that is coming to break open the way for My church to enter into My covenant promises. The angel will come so quickly that people will feel as though they were transported into My purpose. Behold, I send forth My angel on the earth, for My purpose shall be released. People will blink their eyes, and when they open, they will be in their new purposes; the breakthrough will have happened."

I immediately thought of Revelation 22:16, "I, Jesus, have sent My angel to give you this testimony for the churches. I am the Root and the Offspring of David, and the Bright Morning Star."...

...This breakthrough is going to take people out of a narrow church focus and put them into a Kingdom focus, where it's the whole church of Christ receiving, not just a segment....

This is the angel of Jesus Himself, preparing His church to enter into the Kingdom. This is the key to the breakthrough that is coming. It's not about revival. It's about a generation inheriting the promises so they can bring Jesus His reward. This is not something that will begin and end here on earth. This is an outpouring and release of glory that will not end until eternity....

"One who breaks open the way will go up before them; they will break through the gate and go out. Their king will pass through before them, the LORD at their head" (Micah 2:13).[3]

What—or rather, *whom*—are these angels breaking a way for? For the King of glory Himself. He comes to show both mercy and judgment. Therefore, we need to "speak and act as those who are going to be judged by the law that gives freedom, because judgment without mercy will be shown to anyone who has not been merciful. Mercy triumphs over judgment!" (James 2:12–13, NIV).

Angels stand ready to transport God's mercy as well as His judgment. Again, the key that releases them to act is the prayers of Spirit-filled believers. What does it look like when angels bring mercy and judgment?

We see it illustrated in the vivid words of John's revelation:

> Another angel came and stood at the altar, holding a golden censer; and much incense was given to him, so that he might add it to the prayers of all the saints on the golden altar which was before the throne. And the smoke of the incense, with the prayers of the saints, went up before God out of the angel's hand.
>
> Then the angel took the censer and filled it with the fire of the altar, and threw it to the earth; and there followed peals of thunder and sounds and flashes of lightning and an earthquake.
>
> And the seven angels who had the seven trumpets prepared themselves to sound them.
>
> —Revelation 8:3–6

The vision goes on to portray a variety of destructive judgments that are released on the earth. Revelation 16 describes them some more: "Then I heard a loud voice from the temple, saying to the seven angels, 'Go and pour out on the earth the seven bowls of the wrath of God'" (Rev. 16:1).

Here's the pattern. First, the angels gather the praise and prayers of the saints, which are mingled with incense. Second, the prayers and incense are set on fire from the flame on the altar, then put into a censer and waved before God's throne. Third, the fire is thrown back down on the earth. (What goes up must come down.)

The angels are involved at every step of the process, from gathering together the prayers, to igniting them with holy fire so that they become smoking and tangible, to issuing fiery judgments upon the earth from which the prayers arose. Prayer goes up, and answers come down, accompanied by lightning and noise.

Prayers issue forth from those who have received and who will receive God's mercy. God, without compromising His mercy, eradicates all that opposes Him—both operations facilitated by angels, angels, and more angels.

Meantime, God's people on Earth do not have to worry. They will be hidden in His day of wrath. They have cried out for their cities and they have cried out for justice, and they will be saved because of their obedience, their blood-bought righteousness, and their humility. They have asked for God's mercy before His angels cast the fiery rain of judgment on the earth, and they will receive it. The prophet Zephaniah summed it all up:

> Gather yourselves together, yes, gather, O nation without shame, before the decree takes effect—the day passes like the chaff—before the burning anger of the LORD comes upon you, before the day of the LORD's anger comes upon you. Seek the LORD, all you humble of the earth who have carried out His ordinances; seek righteousness, seek humility. Perhaps you will be hidden in the day of the LORD's anger.
>
> —Zephaniah 2:1–3

The Lord gives time for His people to gather themselves together and to call on His name before the Day of Judgment arrives. It's important for us to know how we fit into the picture. We pray the prayers. The angels do God's bidding. His will is that justice will be served. Angels of destruction execute His plan. We are in the path of destruction, but we can count on God's angels of protection to hide us from God's wrath.

We're talking about the End Times here, but we can find application to our daily prayer walk as well.

The Mark of Protection

Another assignment of angels is particularly interesting to intercessors. It is this—the angels of destruction will know which people to skip over because those individuals will bear a mark on their foreheads. Ezekiel saw this played out:

> Then the glory of the God of Israel went up from the cherub on which it had been, to the threshold of the temple. And He called to the man clothed in linen at whose loins was the writing case. The LORD said to him, "Go through the midst of the city, even through the midst of Jerusalem, and put a mark on the foreheads of the men who sigh and groan over all the abominations which are being committed in its midst."
>
> But to the others He said in my hearing, "Go through the city after him and strike; do not let your eye have pity and do not spare. Utterly slay old men, young men, maidens, little children, and women, but do not touch any man on whom is the mark; and you shall start from My sanctuary." So they started with the elders who were before the temple.
>
> —Ezekiel 9:3–6

To whom were the orders being given? They were being given to angels. God gave them assignments. The first wave of angels was commissioned to set a "mark" upon the foreheads of those who "sigh and groan"—in other words, those who pray for relief from the vileness around them. The "mark," some people believe, is in the shape of a cross, because the Hebrew word for "mark" is *taw*, the final letter of their alphabet, which in ancient times used to resemble an *X*. The intercessors, who sigh and weep and groan for the abominations and sins they see around them, will find themselves identified by angelic intervention—thereby consecrated and preserved as a righteous remnant.

This isn't just pie in the sky by-and-by. It's *now*. I remember a gathering I was in one time. God's manifest presence came strongly. Angelic activity was going on in the room. And do you know what happened? A good number of people started noticing glowing crosses on their foreheads. This really happened. We were being marked ahead of time (by angels, most likely) to show us God's pattern.

Our assignment is simple, and it's vital. *Pray.* Pray according to the will of God as revealed to us through His Word and through His servants the angels.

The angels' assignments, although they vary from moment to moment (as do our prayers), are vital to their overall assignment to perform God's bidding.

We're knit together, angels and humans, all servants of the living God.

Lord God, may the veil that separates the eternal from the temporal, the supernatural and the natural, keep on getting thinner and thinner! We welcome heaven's army into our earthly sphere, into the regions over which we have been given jurisdiction. We call forth the angels who watch, who report, who heal, and who deliver. We invite angels to join us in our praise and worship. We expect to see the outcome of the work of angels of breakthrough and protection. We enter into deep intercession with worship. Awaken our senses. Today, send forth Your angels to intervene. [Make it personal. Go out on a limb and ask God to send His angels to you in an unusual way.]
In Jesus's name, amen.

All glory, laud, and honor,
To thee, Redeemer, King,
To whom the lips of children
Made sweet hosannas ring:
Thou art the King of Israel,
Thou David's royal Son,
Who in the Lord's name comest,
The King and blessed One.
The company of angels
Are praising thee on high,
And mortal men and all things
Created make reply:
The people of the Hebrews
With palms before thee went;
Our praise and pray'r and anthems
Before thee we present.[1]

ELEVEN

The Work of Angels and the Nation of Israel

A ngels know the land of Israel better than you know your own neighborhood. They've been there for so long, they seem to have left their footprints everywhere you look. They're still patrolling the skies and the alleyways of the Holy Land, making sure that the divine will of God is accomplished. As I will explain in the following pages, angels and Israel are inseparable.

We see angels throughout the history of the Jewish people, including their pre-Hebrew history contained in the pages of the Bible. We can claim this shared history, too, because our Old Testament comes directly from the Hebrew Scriptures.[2] The first mention of angels appears as early as Genesis 3, where angels were posted to guard the gates of the Garden of Eden. Then, through book after book, whether it's a prophetic message or a royal accounting of a military battle, we see angels everywhere.

We know two archangels by names that came from their Hebrew names: Gabriel and Michael. (*Gabri'el* means "man of God," and *Mikha'el* means "one who is as God.") Many of our names for the different kinds of angels come from Hebrew roots. For example, *cherub* (plural, *cherubim*) comes from the Hebrew *kerubh*. The phrase *Yahweh yosebh hakkerubhim* is translated into English as, "Yahweh seated upon the cherubim," and it most often refers to the design of the ark of the covenant. It can be found in 1 Samuel 4:4; 2 Samuel 6:2; Isaiah 37:16; and the first verses of the eightieth and ninety-ninth psalms.[3] It's easy to see that angels and God's chosen people, Israel, belong together.

However, what's actually important isn't Israel or angels—it's the Messiah Yeshua—the Lord Jesus Himself. He was born there. He loves the people of the entire world, but His heart is particularly focused on Israel, the land of His birth, death, resurrection—and eventual final return. It seems that, like the landowner and his servants in the story Jesus told in Luke 19:13, He has left His angels with the instruction to "occupy until I return." They are faithful to obey Him. Until the end, the angels will always be "preparing the way of the Lord." They exist to serve Him.

Biblical Angelic Encounters in the Holy Land

God is the same yesterday, today, and forever. And what He did before, He does again. History is His story, and He likes to weave together wonderful patterns and themes, which can show us what He may well do again in our own time.

As I have mentioned earlier in the book, God's angels tend to specialize. Like any specialist, they stick with the same sorts of tasks. Therefore, we can expect God and His angels to employ some of the same strategies in our day as they are on record as using in the past. To illustrate what I mean, I have collected a handful of good examples from the history of Israel.

Gideon and the angel

There was much conflict during the period of time after the Israelites crossed into Canaan. To preserve the nation, God sent a series of leaders called judges. One of the most unlikely ones was Gideon. Here's how he found out about the assignment God had for him: "Now it came about when the sons of Israel cried to the LORD on account of Midian...the angel of the LORD came and sat under the oak that was in Ophrah, which belonged to Joash the Abiezrite as his son Gideon was beating out wheat in the wine press in order to save it from the Midianites. The angel of the Lord appeared to him and said to him, 'The Lord is with you, O valiant warrior'" (Judg. 6:6, 11–12).

Angel or no angel, Gideon was not convinced. These were threatening times, and he was *not* a noted warrior. To be sure that this messenger was from God, he asked him to wait for him to prepare an offering.

> So Gideon said to Him, "If now I have found favor in Your sight, then show me a sign that it is You who speak with me. Please do not depart from here, until I come back to You, and bring out my offering and lay it before You."
>
> And He said, "I will remain until you return."
>
> Then Gideon went in and prepared a young goat and unleavened bread from an ephah of flour; he put the meat in a basket and the broth in a pot, and brought them out to him under the oak and presented them.
>
> The angel of God said to him, "Take the meat and the unleavened bread and lay them on this rock, and pour out the broth." And he did so. Then the angel of the Lord put out the end of the staff that was in his hand and touched the meat and the unleavened bread; and fire sprang up from the rock and consumed the meat and the unleavened bread. Then the angel of the Lord vanished from his sight.
>
> When Gideon saw that he was the angel of the Lord, he said, "Alas, O Lord God! For now I have seen the angel of the Lord face to face."
>
> —Judges 6:17–22

That should have been an indisputable sign, but Gideon needed a lot more convincing. So God gave him every confirmation he required, and He also gave him detailed instructions as to how to prevail over the Midianites in a strategy involving a select company of only three hundred men who would hide their torches under clay jars!

Only God could get the credit for all of this. His angel first visited Gideon as he was winnowing the harvest. (Angelic encounters and times of harvest and times of victory all flow together.) Then, when Gideon's army blew their shofars and shattered the clay jars that hid their torches, it was a picture of how you and I can proclaim God's victory and let His light shine—if we are unified and obedient. God is still in the same business today—the victory business.

God heard the Israelites' cry for help, and He sent an angel to notify a leader and help him muster the necessary troops, and then He helped him go to battle and win.

(An important note: we must realize that angelic involvement does not guarantee that we will be whisked away from trouble. While they do come to deliver us from our fears, they do not necessarily remove the dangerous circumstances. When they do come to help us, it is usually so that we can stand strong and fight better and come out on top.)

Abraham and the angels

Since childhood, you've heard the story of the angelic delegation that visited Abraham and Sarah by the oaks of Mamre. "Three men," who are assumed to have been angels, arrived and spoke to Abraham. He welcomed them hospitably, and soon he discovered that they were no ordinary travelers. The spokesman declared, with the authority of God Himself, "I will surely return to you at this time next year; and behold, Sarah your wife will have a son" (Gen. 18:10). Then he seemed to read Sarah's thoughts and said, "Why did Sarah laugh, saying, 'Shall I indeed bear a child, when I am so old?' Is anything too difficult for the LORD? At the appointed time I will return to you, at this time next year, and Sarah will have a son" (Gen. 18:13–14).

Those angelic visitors weren't the only ones in Abraham's story. Earlier, Hagar, Sarah's maid, had had a visit from an angel when she was still pregnant with Ishmael. You will remember that the reason she was pregnant is that the still-barren Sarah (known as Sarai at the time) had given her to her husband, Abraham, in hopes of achieving a fulfillment of God's promise of an heir. Hagar became pregnant right away, and her relationship with her mistress deteriorated as a result, to the point that she fled. That's where the angel comes in:

> Now the angel of the LORD found her by a spring of water in the wilderness, by the spring on the way to Shur. He said, "Hagar, Sarai's maid, where have you come from and where are you going?"
>
> And she said, "I am fleeing from the presence of my mistress Sarai."
>
> Then the angel of the LORD said to her, "Return to your mistress, and submit yourself to her authority." Moreover, the angel of the LORD said to her, "I will greatly multiply your descendants so that they will be too many to count."
>
> The angel of the LORD said to her further, "Behold, you are with child, and you will bear a son; and you shall call his name Ishmael, because the LORD has given heed to your affliction. He will be a wild donkey of a man, his hand will be against everyone, and everyone's hand will be against him; and he will live to the east of all his brothers."
>
> —Genesis 16:7–12

Both angelic messages came true. Sarah did become pregnant, and she bore Isaac, just as the angel had said. Now Abraham had two sons. Sarah's relationship with Hagar did not improve, however. Eventually, when Ishmael was a young teenager, Sarah provoked Abraham to send Hagar and Ishmael away. Abraham and Sarah never saw them again, but God was looking after them, in order to fulfill His promises to Abraham—and to Hagar:

> She departed and wandered about in the wilderness of Beersheba. When the water in the skin was used up, she left the boy under one of the bushes. Then she went and sat down opposite him, about a bowshot away, for she said, "Do not let me see the boy die." And she sat opposite him, and lifted up her voice and wept.
>
> God heard the lad crying; and the angel of God called to Hagar from heaven and said to her, "What is the matter with you, Hagar? Do not fear, for God has heard the voice of the lad where he is.

Arise, lift up the lad, and hold him by the hand, for I will make a great nation of him."

Then God opened her eyes and she saw a well of water; and she went and filled the skin with water and gave the lad a drink.

—Genesis 21:14–19

Israel's patriarch Abraham and his family encountered angels often. Besides the accounts above, we read about the story of Abraham's nephew Lot and the angels at Sodom. And then there's the story of Abraham's near-sacrifice of Isaac. An angel was involved in that one, too, providing the ram and instructing Abraham as to what to do.

Then they came to the place of which God had told him; and Abraham built the altar there and arranged the wood, and bound his son Isaac and laid him on the altar, on top of the wood.

Abraham stretched out his hand and took the knife to slay his son. But the angel of the LORD called to him from heaven and said, "Abraham, Abraham!"

And he said, "Here I am."

He said, "Do not stretch out your hand against the lad, and do nothing to him; for now I know that you fear God, since you have not withheld your son, your only son, from Me."

—Genesis 22:9–12

Angels guided and preserved Abraham and his family over and over again. God wanted to achieve His plan to establish His chosen people, the Jews. He also wanted to establish and bless the other people groups who arose from Abraham's seed. It's incredible to think about how it happened.

God's promises to the offspring of the patriarch Abraham, uttered through His angels, remain valid, even though, by and large, the people of the Middle East have to this day failed to realize how much of the promise is fulfilled in Yeshua, the Lord Jesus. The Jews don't believe that He's the Messiah they have been waiting for, and the Arab world doesn't realize that they even need a Savior.

That fact should compel us to our knees again and again. Jesus said, "I have other sheep, which are not of this fold; I must bring them also, and they will hear My voice; and they will become one flock with one shepherd" (John 10:16). We who have ourselves been "grafted in" to the vine of Israel (as Paul wrote in Romans 11) can ask God to command His angels to break through the darkness all over the Middle East.

Daniel and the archangel

The story of Daniel gives us a powerful glimpse of the invisible angelic battle in the heavenlies over this region of the world. He was, you will remember, an Israelite in exile in Babylon. He longed for the day when he and his fellow exiles would be able to return to their own land. One time, after he had been fasting and praying for three weeks, an angel appeared to him:

> In those days, I, Daniel, had been mourning for three entire weeks. I did not eat any tasty food, nor did meat or wine enter my mouth, nor did I use any ointment at all until the entire three weeks were completed.
>
> On the twenty-fourth day of the first month, while I was by the bank of the great river, that is, the Tigris, I lifted my eyes and looked, and behold, there was a certain man dressed in linen, whose waist was girded with a belt of pure gold of Uphaz. His body also was like beryl, his face had the appearance of lightning, his eyes were like flaming torches, his arms and feet like the gleam of polished bronze, and the sound of his words like the sound of a tumult.
>
> —Daniel 10:2–6

This angel, as we have seen in many other instances, caused great fear. The men who were with Daniel fled, even though they couldn't see the angel or hear his words. And Daniel himself was overcome:

> So I was left alone and saw this great vision; yet no strength was left in me, for my natural color turned to a deathly pallor, and I retained no strength. But I heard the sound of his words; and as

soon as I heard the sound of his words, I fell into a deep sleep on my face, with my face to the ground.

Then behold, a hand touched me and set me trembling on my hands and knees. He said to me, "O Daniel, man of high esteem, understand the words that I am about to tell you and stand upright, for I have now been sent to you." And when he had spoken this word to me, I stood up trembling.

—Daniel 10:8–11

The angel proceeded to explain what was happening and what was going to happen, and in order to do so, he had to make it possible for Daniel to withstand his powerful presence:

Then he said to me, "Do not be afraid...I have come in response to your words. But the prince of the kingdom of Persia was withstanding me for twenty-one days; then behold, Michael, one of the chief princes, came to help me, for I had been left there with the kings of Persia. Now I have come to give you an understanding of what will happen to your people in the latter days, for the vision pertains to the days yet future."

When he had spoken to me according to these words, I turned my face toward the ground and became speechless. And behold, one who resembled a human being was touching my lips; then I opened my mouth and spoke and said to him who was standing before me, "O my lord, as a result of the vision anguish has come upon me, and I have retained no strength. For how can such a servant of my lord talk with such as my lord? As for me, there remains just now no strength in me, nor has any breath been left in me."

Then this one with human appearance touched me again and strengthened me. He said, "O man of high esteem, do not be afraid. Peace be with you; take courage and be courageous!"

Now as soon as he spoke to me, I received strength and said, "May my lord speak, for you have strengthened me."

—Daniel 10:12–19

No wonder Daniel could hardly stand to listen. This angel was probably none other than the archangel Gabriel, and he was explaining what the most superior of all archangels, Michael, was going to do. (Largely because of Daniel's account, the Jews since his time have claimed Michael as the guardian angel of Israel.) "Then he said, 'Do you understand why I came to you? But I shall now return to fight against the prince of Persia; so I am going forth, and behold, the prince of Greece is about to come. However, I will tell you what is inscribed in the writing of truth. Yet there is no one who stands firmly with me against these forces except Michael your prince'" (Dan. 10:20–21).

The "prince of Persia" was the evil principality who ruled over that region. Together, Gabriel and Michael would withstand not only that principality but also the "prince of Greece." God sent them in response to Daniel's fervent prayers.

Modern-Day Angelic Encounters in the Holy Land

Angels have intervened—often openly—at every crucial juncture in the history of Israel. We have had a chance to see this firsthand, especially since the reestablishment in 1948 of the state of Israel. The Six-Day War in June of 1967 was swift and successful, adding the Gaza Strip, the Sinai Peninsula, the West Bank, and the Golan Heights to the territory that Israel had already reclaimed. Then came the Yom Kippur War.

Yom Kippur War

The Yom Kippur War of 1973 could have meant the end of Israel as a state. Egypt, Jordan, Iraq, and Syria joined forces to mount a surprise attack and, they hoped, annihilate the Jews.

Lance Lambert, an English pastor and intercessor who has long been a friend of Israel, happened to be in Jerusalem when the war broke out, and he includes an account of angelic intervention in his book *Battle for Israel,* which is now out of print. First, some background:

> People think of the 1967 Six-Day War as a miracle, but it was nothing compared with the Yom Kippur War, and in the years that

lie ahead, when the whole truth comes out, we shall see that it was beyond all reason that Israel was not annihilated.

A few weeks after the war, I heard Golda Meir [the prime minister of Israel] say, "For the first time in our twenty-five year history, we thought we might have lost." Before then I had never heard a prominent Israeli so much as imply the possibility of defeat or admit to fear. At one point in the war, only ninety battered Israeli tanks stood between the powerful Egyptian army and Tel Aviv, yet Israel was not beaten....

In the Yom Kippur War, which was the first wholly technological war in Middle East history, approximately 4,000 tanks, 900 missile batteries, and even unproved new weapons were thrown into action. Egypt attacked with 3,000 tanks, 2,000 heavy guns, 1,000 aircraft, and 600,000 men.

The regular Israeli garrisons numbered only a few hundred men against the massive tank attack. With their greater numbers, the Egyptians should have been in El Arish, if not in Gaza and Beersheba, within twenty-four hours and then the whole of Israel's heartland would have been exposed. There was nothing to stop them....

Egypt and Syria should have beaten Israel, but they were inexplicably prevented....If they had swept on, the whole of central Israel would have been at their mercy. One Egyptian tank commander said later, "I was only half an hour's drive from the Mitla Pass, and there was nothing to stop me." Yet the fact is he stopped.

Likewise the Syrians should have been in Tiberias on the evening of the first day of the war but they too stopped....Wave after wave of tanks bore down on [the Israeli Golani brigade]. Then when they came to within one mile of the headquarters, they halted. "They saw the Lake of Galilee...they liked the view, and they stopped."[4]

In Lance's account, now we begin to see the hand of God, quite literally:

[An] Israeli captain without any religious beliefs said that at the height of the fighting on the Golan, he looked up into the sky and saw a great, grey hand pressing downwards as if it were holding something back. In my opinion that describes exactly what happened; without the intervention of God, Israel would have been doomed....

The fighting became increasingly severe. Galilee was shelled and the Syrians even used Frog missiles. There were many air raids in the north but then Syria was gradually pushed back. Meanwhile, Egypt was held in the Sinai where the greatest tank battle in world history was fought on Friday, October 19th. Much of the fighting was at such close range that they weren't even able to maneuver the tanks. Jordanian radio described it as "Hell on earth."[5]

Then the prayers began to go up, although not without a struggle:

Many of the Christians in Jerusalem felt that the main purpose of my being delayed there was for prayer....[The warden of the garden tomb of Jesus offered us accommodation in a house there.] It was as if one was at the heart of things. Here was the natural centre for most of the Christians in Jerusalem....I found here as everywhere else, that [genuine corporate prayer] is a lost art....

I was appalled that when Israel was in such great need, even Christian workers and servants of the Lord who had been clearly put there by God and really felt God calling them to pray for all that was going on at the time were unable to pray together in depth....So we held a school of prayer at the height of the war. Our burden was for the dying and wounded, Arab and Jew alike, that they might be saved; for the Israeli people, that the war might be used to turn them to God; for the invaders, that the Lord would paralyze and confuse them, and especially for Jordan, that she would not enter the war.[6]

Lance and his group of intercessors saw their prayers answered, and it didn't take very long. Their fervent prayers included prayers for world leaders, who were deciding whether and how to become involved on both sides of the war. Some Christians, who had been tutored by the late Rees Howells in crisis intercession, felt that the enemy was trying to

precipitate Armageddon. Prayer was not just a good idea; it was *vital*.
Lance continues:

> [Israel's] right to exist and her claim to destiny have always been
> contested. From the very beginning of her history the powers of
> darkness and evil have sought to destroy her from both without
> and within....
>
> Israel represents spiritual realities and values. The Israel of old
> has left us with no great monuments such as the pyramids of ancient
> Egypt, or the great works of art such as the Chinese have left us.
> Instead she has given us the word of God. In this we see her history
> set forth as a living, dynamic relationship with God. This lesson
> is seen both positively at the high points of her spiritual life and
> negatively during those times when she fell away from the Lord.
> God was teaching Israel that everything depends upon a right rela-
> tionship to himself. It is in this way that the whole history of Israel
> is the setting forth of spiritual realities. It is not a matter of secular
> history but the unfolding of God's purpose to save mankind.[7]

I heard another testimony about what happened in the Yom Kippur
War: "In the end, there were three thousand Egyptian tanks coming
up from the Sinai, and the Egyptians heard an enormous, loud, roaring
sound, and they stopped their progress." The Egyptians believed that it
was the sound of hundreds of tanks coming against them. But there were
not hundreds of Israeli tanks coming. The people who gave that testimony believed that God had released His angels and that the roaring
was the sound of it. Israel's troops heard the roaring sound, too. Part of
that battle did not occur. It was stopped in its tracks.

God did it in the time of Abraham. He did it in the time of Gideon.
He did it in the time of Daniel. And He did it at the Yom Kippur War.
Angels are on assignment, and they will be released in response to the
fervent cries of God's people.

The wedding of the church and Israel

Michal Ann and I have always carried what we would call a "core value" regarding God's heart toward Israel. But I didn't teach and preach very much about the subject until I had an experience that I call "the wedding of the church and Israel." I mentioned the experience in my book *The Prophetic Intercessor,* but here I want to give you some more background about the angelic component.

When we were beginning to travel and host some of our own conferences and seminars, we had one at a state park retreat center in Georgia. Immediately prior to this event, I had had a couple of amazing dreams in which I had watched weddings. In the dreams, I was with friends who were working to strengthen the church and who had ties with Israel. When the bride came down the aisle to meet the groom in the dreams, somehow I knew that the groom symbolized Russia and that the bride symbolized Israel. The dream had many aspects; that was just one of them. The dream was a precursor for me to go into the former Soviet Union, specifically Russia, to be part of outreaches to the Jewish people there.

Anyway, back at the retreat center in Georgia, one of the primary themes was Israel. One night, before I was supposed to speak, we were engaged in a time of worship. Suddenly, in an open vision, I saw an unusual-looking angel in the corner of the room of the lodge where we were. I had seen only a few up to that time, so I was puzzled about the clothing that this angel was wearing. The angel was wearing a brilliant white wedding gown. And I heard the angel say, "I have come to release a message on the wedding of the church and Israel."

I stepped forward to give the evening message, and all I know is that I spoke that night well beyond anything I had studied or rehearsed for. I felt as if the angel had created new faith in me and had imparted a kind of knowledge and revelation that I hadn't had before. I spoke at length about the birth of the nation of Israel, the modern-day exodus of the Jews from the lands of the north (Russia and the European countries that had been involved in the Holocaust of World War II) to Israel, and how that exodus was bringing and would continue to bring about the wedding of the church and Israel. Change is coming! It will come to both the church's perspective concerning Israel and Israel's perspective concerning the church.

You can read much more about my involvement in the outworking of the wedding of the church and Israel in chapter 9 of my book *The Prophetic Intercessor,* which is called "Israel, God's Prophetic Calendar," and in my books *Exodus Cry* and *Praying for Israel's Destiny.*

An angel named Israel Awakening

In renewal meetings in Long Island, New York, where I was ministering in December of 2006, I saw something that I had never seen before. During the worship portion of the closing Saturday evening service, I felt something come into the auditorium; it was as though the atmosphere had suddenly shifted. I looked up, and an angel of the Lord manifested itself flying in on the wind and hovering in the air, carrying a shofar. It was dressed in a white, flowing, radiant garment with a gold sash wrapped from one shoulder to the waist. Words were written upon the sash. The words read, "Israel Awakening." As soon as it appeared before me, its appearance departed.

I proceeded to preach my message that night on "Open Heavens and the Ministering Angels." At the close, we went into some extended ministry time. I was waiting for the proper moment to introduce this activity that I had seen during the worship time. Then, again, I felt the atmosphere shift.

At that point, I told the people that an angel named Israel Awakening had been released to bring a spiritual awakening to both the Jewish people (regarding God's purposes within Israel) and to the body of the Messiah, the church of Jesus Christ, concerning her role of supporting Israel in the last days.

A confirmation came immediately—only God can do this. The man who was the host of the meetings then got up and read something he had scribbled on his pad of paper. He too had sensed in worship that an angel had come into the meeting that night to awaken the church to

Israel. We compared our notes—both of us had written down that the name of the angel was Israel Awakening.

So get ready—change *is* coming! Angels are on assignment to both the church and to Israel.

Israel-Hezbollah conflict of 2006

In mid-July through the cease-fire in early August of 2006, news reports were dominated with the conflict between Hezbollah forces, based north of Israel in Lebanon, and the Israeli Air Force and Israeli (ground) Defense Forces.

During that time, Christians in the Western world began to intensify their prayers for Israel. Bill Yount, a prophet based in Maryland who contributed an angel story to chapter 8, had a vision:

> I saw strong angels standing wing-tip to wing-tip on the borders of Israel. Momentarily, I saw a "small break" appear in a demonic black cloud that was hanging over the nation of Israel. As this small break in this cloud appeared, simultaneously the borders of Israel lit up like a flashing green light from Heaven signaling, "We've got 'a Go' for launching!"
>
> Immediately I saw many of these strong angels being released from their duty on the borders of Israel and being sent (as in an emergency) to personally deliver messages to churches all over the world to pray for the peace of Jerusalem.[8]

Do you see how it's all tied together and how the angels play such an important role? Israel, the land of God's promise, is guarded and aided by angel battalions who are released by the prayers of faithful believers everywhere. God's eye is on Israel, and we can expect to see angels, in response to God's bidding, arise to affect events of worldwide significance.

Myriads of Angels

Think about it—the physical city of Jerusalem, the city of David, has actually given its name to the heavenly city in the highest heaven, which is thronged with the countless heavenly host:

> For you have not come [as did the Israelites in the wilderness] to a [material] mountain that can be touched, [a mountain] that is ablaze with fire, and to gloom and darkness and a raging storm, and to the blast of a trumpet and a voice whose words make the listeners beg that nothing more be said to them....
>
> But rather, you have come to Mount Zion, even to *the city of the living God, the heavenly Jerusalem, and to countless multitudes of angels in festal gathering,* and to the church (assembly) of the Firstborn who are registered [as citizens] in heaven, and to the God Who is Judge of all, and to the spirits of the righteous (the redeemed in heaven) who have been made perfect, and to Jesus, the Mediator (Go-between, Agent) of a new covenant, and to the sprinkled blood which speaks [of mercy], a better and nobler and more gracious message than the blood of Abel [which cried out for vengeance].
>
> —Hebrews 12:18–19, 22–24, AMP, emphasis added

So we too join in with the heavenly choirs, worshiping and working to usher in the kingdom of God on Earth, empowered by the Spirit and aided by angels, declaring, "Worthy, *worthy* is the Lamb!"

Lord, we welcome the heavenly army into the earth realm. We lift our prayers and petitions for Your plans, purposes, and destiny to come forth in fullness. May Your kingdom come, and may Your will be done, on Earth as it is in heaven. We welcome the messenger angels who come to release Your word. We welcome the healing angels who usher in Your signs and wonders. We applaud those angels who battle evil foes and those who gather in the harvest from the ripe fields. We are eternally grateful for the angels of Your presence, who bring us glimpses of Your heavenly glory and who remind us of Your eternal purposes. Come, Lord Jesus! In Your great name and for Your sake, amen.

Rejoice in glorious hope! Jesus the Judge shall come,
And take His servants up to their eternal home.
We soon shall hear th' archangel's voice;
The trump of God shall sound, rejoice![1]

TWELVE

Angels, the Harvest, and the End Times

Trumpets are sounded to rally troops. They also awaken people or signal the start of an event. When you see or hear angels with trumpets, you know that divine proclamations are being made. Something new, something important, is being released.

I remember seeing angels with trumpets during a Passion for Jesus conference in Kansas City. We were in the Music Hall, which has a heart-shaped ceiling, in the midst of some radical worship. I looked up with my eyes open, and I saw angels; they were blowing horns. They would blow them repeatedly, and when they did, something was released from their trumpets that looked like honeybees being sent forth, carrying something golden, which they took out over the people and dropped down on them. I think they were dropping the anointing on the people. I felt that apostolic mandates were being released. The atmosphere was absolutely *electric* with praise and worship. The angels joined with us, and we joined with them. That night, it seemed that the angels were trumpeting and announcing, initiating something new, a new dimension of anointing and of God's glory.

More anointing. When God sends angels, with or without trumpets, to proclaim, release, and anoint, what should our response be? Ian Andrews, who is the director of the International Association of Healing

Ministries, tells how he was given an assignment after angels came to perform their assignment. Ian is from Great Britain, but he ministers much of the year in the United States. On this occasion in 1992, he was in Minneapolis. As he spoke from the platform, the people in the audience, with their eyes open, saw behind him seven angels. He wrote to me about it:

> [The seven angels] appeared behind me on a platform with golden anointing bowls in their hands....I was given the task of pouring out seven anointings in those meetings: salvations, healings, refreshings, baptisms in the Holy Spirit, deliverances, miracles, and new vision for the purposes of God....It was the start of a fresh move of God in Minneapolis for that season....This activity of the Spirit then broke out again in another hungry church in the same region of the city, including angelic activity, a couple of years later. Perhaps it was the same angels who were at work in these regional demonstrations of God's glory on earth.[2]

As God accomplishes His End-Times purposes in the earth, we will see increases in angelic activity, especially in the realm of releasing anointing and making proclamations. Later in this chapter, you will read more about the way God pairs up His assignments to believers with the assignments He gives His angels on a worldwide scale. First, let's review the range of assignments that He can give to His angels.

Angels on Review

In the previous chapters of this book, we've explored angelic assignments. God sends angels to:

- Minister God's presence
- Deliver God's message
- Release dreams, revelation, and understanding
- Give guidance and direction
- Bring forth deliverance

- Grant protection
- Usher the saints to heaven at the time of death
- Impart strength
- Release healing

Also, as they were doing in Kansas City on that memorable occasion I described above, angels bring heaven to Earth by means of praise and worship, and they announce the coming of Christ's glorious kingdom. They mingle with God's saints on Earth as they praise Him, "saying with a loud voice, 'Worthy is the Lamb that was slain to receive power and riches and wisdom and might and honor and glory and blessing'" (Rev. 5:12). In that context, we sometimes see them or hear them blow their trumpets and lay claim to territory for the King.

In addition, night and day, angels are *divine watchers*. They look into the historical affairs of man. (See Daniel 4:13, 17.) They watch, listen, and respond—sometimes by destroying God's enemies outright (Acts 12:23). They pronounce and execute God's judgments over all the earth, and they do it without partiality (1 Tim. 5:21). (See both Old and New Testament passages, such as Genesis 19:11; Exodus 12:23–30; and Revelation 16:17ff.) They pour out bowls. They sound forth more blasts from their heavenly trumpets.

With all they do, you'd think we'd notice them more often, wouldn't you? The angelic population throngs the heavens, but we earthbound folks get only glimpses of them. What are the angels doing today? We want to have some idea about their assignments, because we want to be "on the same page" with them. The church is collaborating with the angels in the outworking of the great finale of God's eternal plan.

In time, you know, many of them will put down their trumpets so they can pick up their sickles and their scythes. A major part of their duty will involve the End-Time harvest. In other words, they serve as *reapers and gatherers*. They gather up the harvest in its ripeness and transport it to God's heavenly storehouses. (See Revelation 14:14–19.) We know that they will gather up the tares, weeds, and brambles, too—to be burned (Matt. 13:25–30). They gather up the souls of men for the time of God's judgment:

> Then I saw another angel flying in midair, and he had the eternal gospel to proclaim to those who live on the earth—to every nation, tribe, language and people. He said in a loud voice, "Fear God and give him glory, because the hour of his judgment has come. Worship him who made the heavens, the earth, the sea and the springs of water."
>
> —Revelation 14:6–7, NIV

> Then I looked, and behold, a white cloud, and sitting on the cloud was one like a son of man, having a golden crown on His head and a sharp sickle in His hand. And another angel came out of the temple, crying out with a loud voice to Him who sat on the cloud, "Put in your sickle and reap, for the hour to reap has come, because the harvest of the earth is ripe."
>
> Then He who sat on the cloud swung His sickle over the earth, and the earth was reaped.
>
> And another angel came out of the temple which is in heaven, and he also had a sharp sickle. Then another angel, the one who has power over fire, came out from the altar; and he called with a loud voice to him who had the sharp sickle, saying, "Put in your sharp sickle and gather the clusters from the vine of the earth, because her grapes are ripe."
>
> So the angel swung his sickle to the earth and gathered the clusters from the vine of the earth, and threw them into the great wine press of the wrath of God.
>
> —Revelation 14:14–19

Angels That Gather

As the End Times approach and warfare intensifies, you can expect to hear more reports of "sightings" of angels operating in their End-Times assignments. Paul Keith Davis reports on such an experience. He and his wife, Wanda, had been invited to participate in the dedication service of the Vineyard Christian Fellowship in Albany, Oregon:

On Friday, October 17, Wanda and I flew to Albany to join our friends Bob Jones, Bobby Conner, Don and Christine Potter, and others [who] were involved in the services. The whole day was spent on airplanes and in airports. It was not a positive spiritual atmosphere. The day certainly did not prepare me for what transpired the moment I stepped into the sanctuary on that Friday evening.…

The service had already begun by the time we arrived. Don Potter was leading worship, and the people were fully engaged in the service. Instantly, with my first step into the auditorium, I was seeing both the natural and spiritual realms at the same time. My natural eyes were seeing people as they worshiped, but my spiritual eyes were open to see the Spirit's realm. With open eyes, I clearly saw angels standing from one corner of the building across the back to the other corner.

Each angel appeared to be about six to seven feet tall. They were standing approximately six feet apart, and they each wore a white robe that reached to their feet. They were each watching the podium as Don Potter was leading worship. Some had golden belts that seemed to be made of a rope-like material and others had golden sashes that draped across their chests. Their countenances were compassionate and caring. Some from heaven's host are fierce and overwhelming in appearance, but these seemed tender and loving.

My first question was, "Who are they?" The answer came immediately and emphatically. The Spirit said, "They are angels that gather." To my knowledge, I had never before heard that expression. Angels that gather were a fresh revelation to me. As I took the seat next to the pastor, I advised him that there were angels standing across the back of his church. He asked what kind of angels, and I firmly and authoritatively stated, "They are angels that gather," although that phrase was made known to me only moments before. I needed a Scripture to confirm my statement to the pastor. Fortunately, I was able to discover the biblical affirmation of this reality in Matthew 13, [which speaks of] the latter-day generation and outlines our provision for the end-time confrontation.... It is a clear outline of the spiritual conflict that will exist in the days immediately preceding His return....

> And He said, "The one who sows the good seed is the Son of Man, and the field is the world; and as for the good seed, these are the sons of the Kingdom; and the tares are the sons of the evil one; and the enemy who sowed them is the devil, and the harvest is the end of the age; and the reapers are angels. So just as the tares are gathered up and burned with fire, so shall it be at the end of the age.
>
> "The Son of Man will send forth His angels, and they will gather out of His kingdom all stumbling blocks, and those who commit lawlessness, and will throw them into the furnace of fire; in that place there will be weeping and gnashing of teeth. Then the righteous will shine forth as the sun in the kingdom of their Father. He who has ears, let him hear." (Matthew 13:37–43)

...Angels that gather will not only collect the wheat into the barn but also extract stumbling blocks that interfere with the flourishing of God's Kingdom.[3]

When you hear stories like this, you know that the Lord's army is on the move. His manifest presence (which, remember, is ushered in by His angels) precedes His actual coming. Jesus *is* coming soon.

It's the angels who are His advance guard as well as His enlisted troops. Just as the troops in any army each have specific marching orders, so do the angels. That's why we see them in so many roles, all centered around one primary goal: to defeat the enemy and his forces, who were once part of their own number, and to bring in the rule and reign of God, the Captain of the Host.

This is spiritual warfare. This bright army is amazingly strong. They are relentless. They bind and capture. Battle by battle, they win the war. In the time to come, we will celebrate with them the greatest victory of all time.

It's About Jesus!

As I've said already, it isn't about angels—it's about Jesus Himself. Angels help us know where He is. Wherever Jesus is, the angels are.

Jesus is our Bridegroom, and the church is His bride. With John in the Book of Revelation, we say, "The Spirit and the bride say, 'Come!'" (Rev. 22:17). Our invitation, often repeated, opens the way for more angelic activity than ever. And that's what is needed before the final, cataclysmic, great coming of the Lord when all His heavenly host will be His escort.

Two armies

The late Rolland Smith had many experiences with angels—so many that I can't share about all of them. But I want to close this chapter and this book with his incredible account of what happened to him in the mid-1980s.[4] His story will both illustrate what I've been trying to explain about angels and expand your vision for what God is doing in the earth as the End Times draw near.

He starts by portraying the two armies of God:

> The army of God is actually two armies. One part is in heaven. The other part is on earth. Even though only on rare occasions have people been allowed to see the heavenly army, it does exist. In these last days, God is revealing His strategies concerning the cooperation of these two armies.
>
> Jacob saw these two armies in a vision. One of them was a mighty host of angels (the heavenly army), and the other was Jacob's family (the earthly army). To commemorate the vision, he named the place where the vision occurred *Mahanaim*, which means "a double army." This place had great significance since it was the "reentry point" of Jacob's return to Canaan, the border of the land of promise. It was here that Jacob sent word to his estranged brother, Esau, [to say] that he was coming home and desired to be reconciled with him.
>
> David camped at the same location when his son, Absalom, rebelled and tried to take over the kingdom. Here again, there were two armies, but this time two armies of Israel were fighting each

other. What a picture! The church must, in like manner, revisit *Mahanaim* if we are going to experience the uniting of the body of Christ under the mighty Son of David, King Jesus, and if we are going to see the heavenly army take their position of protection over us, God's heritage.

Rolland goes on to tell about what happened to him in 1984 when he was on a long trip from Sweden, where he was living at the time, to Yugoslavia. Before he left Sweden, he stopped in a suburb of Stockholm to spend some time praying in an apartment that was being renovated for the use of a man who had a worldwide prophetic intercessory ministry.

While he was praying there, the presence of the Lord came upon him so strongly that he was pressed flat to the floor on his face. He could not look up or open his eyes, and he "became acutely aware that three angelic beings were standing in the room." He said he was conscious of their physical appearance and even of their thoughts, and he was overwhelmed with joy and peace as they began to praise the Lord Jesus.

They shared many things with me. One told of all the battles they had fought side-by-side with the saints in other generations, including Joshua and David. As they spoke, my mind seemed to be instantly filled with understanding. I felt numb as the thought permeated my soul that I was in the presence of beings who had never died, but had lived throughout the entire history of the people of God.

The mind-boggling picture began to come into focus of how the armies of heaven are fighting alongside of God's sons and daughters here on earth. As I very timidly struggled to form a question that was forcing itself into my mind, I noticed a wariness on their faces similar to what I had seen on the faces of those who had spent long months on the front lines of major wars. They looked like battle-scarred veterans. I finally managed to whisper the nagging question, "Why haven't we won the war against the forces of Satan in the earth?"

The answer they gave was embedded in my mind forever, "We have helped God's children to win the same territories many times, only to have them lost again to the devil and his forces." Their answer stung me to shame as my thoughts raced back over some of the dismal events in the history of the church, and the many glorious visitations of God's grace upon His people. Many times there have been dynamic expansions of the work of God among the nations, only to be followed by dark periods of coldness, hardness, rebellion, schisms, and devilish deceptions.

I could feel the quiet, steel-like strength of their never-ending vigilance and patience on the battlefield, as they stood motionless, waiting respectfully for my response. Their holy stillness and inner peace gave me strength to summon courage to speak one last time. It was a question that had risen up to torment my soul over and over all my life. It now came forcibly to my mind. "When will the war be over?" I asked hesitantly. As I posed this question, I was thinking of the promises in the Word of God when all the hordes of hell are finally vanquished, and all authorities and powers put under the feet of our Lord Jesus Christ, when His kingdom will reign supreme over all the earth.

The answer came from the spokesman of the three, who had been standing just above my head, "The church on earth does not know or seem to care to understand what the invisible armies in heaven are doing. They are very preoccupied with their celebrations and feasts....When the church comprehends what we are doing and is ready to fight together with us in complete obedience to our glorious Head, Jesus Christ, then we will win the war."

Rolland wrote that several other brothers came into the room at that point. They couldn't see or hear anything, but they knew that something very powerful was occurring. Rolland tried to explain, but he was too overwhelmed to do so.

He continued on his trip to Yugoslavia, accompanied by an intercessor friend named Oke and another Swedish man, as well as a Yugoslavian brother. In that country, they traveled together in a small yellow car. After traveling on the main highway to a series of meetings, they decided to return by back roads, because the main highway was so congested and dangerous. Soon they were lost, but they redeemed the time by praying for and blessing every place they passed, feeling that this was perhaps the purpose of their detour. The presence of God filled the little car. Rolland continues:

Suddenly, the Spirit of God came over me as I sat in the left rear seat. I began to pray in a language I did not understand and had never prayed in before. As I prayed, it seemed as if a curtain moved away, and the heavens opened up. There before me was an enormous host of angels. As far as the eye could see in all directions, the heavens were filled with angels. I lost all sense of where I was and seemed to be lifted up into the very presence of these angels. I could see in great detail.

There was much activity everywhere with singing, shouting, and a kaleidoscope of brilliant lights of every color flaring out into the heavens. Yet in spite of all this flurry of motion, there was a strange sense of order. There was no confusion.

The Lord Jesus Christ was in the center of it all. It was almost a shock to see Him. So striking was His appearance that He dominated everything. The look on His face was so filled with expression it was as if I could see deep into His soul. I saw an expression of joy, yet it seemed to be mixed with deep, sorrowful compassion. I had an unmistakable feeling that He had waited for a very long time for this day to come, and now He was ready to act.

The air was filled with anticipation that something extraordinary was about to happen. I thought I was witnessing the throne room of God, yet Jesus was not on a throne. He stood at a large desk, similar to a bar of justice in a courtroom where the judge sits. Behind Him was a huge bookshelf lined with volumes of very large books. They were very old books, bound with thick leather covers, securely locked. The Lord took one of these books, laid it on the desk, and unlocked it.

He then began to take the pages from the book, one at a time. As He took a page, a trumpet blast was sounded, and a band of mighty angels came forward and stood before the Lord in rapt attention. They were enormously powerful and beautiful beings. With great solemnity, the Lord Jesus Christ presented each band with a page from the book. The Lord spoke briefly to the group and commanded them to go quickly. Then, with a mighty flash of light, the angels flew away.

This process was repeated hundreds of times, with each band of angels being given a single page from the book and sent forth by the Lord. This continued until every page was removed from the large book. Then, Jesus would turn and select another of the strange ancient chronicles, open it very carefully, and begin to give out each page to the summoned band of His faithful heavenly servants.

As I watched, I continued to utter the strange language. The thought went through my mind that the Holy Spirit was speaking out of my mouth the same words that were going out of the mouth of the Lord. I was transfixed. It seemed like I was not even breathing. Time must have stood still. What I was witnessing should have taken hours to complete.

Finally, one large section of what must have been hundreds of thousands, perhaps millions of angels, were all sent forth. It became clear that a whole army of angels had been dispatched by the Lord into different parts of the earth. I shuddered as a huge, awesome angel came forth and blew a loud, long blast on a golden trumpet. This caused millions of angels on two sides of the Lord to change their positions. There was a mighty shift, and about half of the angels who remained stood directly in front of the Lord Jesus. It was evident that this was a distinct army of angels, with recognizable leaders. They stood in perfect order, row upon row, reaching to the horizon.

The Lord of Hosts began to repeat just what He had done with the first army of angels. A large, thick book was opened, and with much gravity, the Lord would take a page and give it to a selected band of angels. They would be sent forth with very specific directions.

By some means, I seemed to be brought much closer to the scene immediately around the Lord Jesus. As this happened, I was able to actually look at the pages as they were handed out by the Lord. The paper was very old parchment. The loose-leaf volumes were thick, with richly carved leather-bound covers. It looked like it had been written a very long time ago. As the pages became visible to me, I noticed that there were maps drawn on about half of the page, with handwritten notes filling the rest of the space. The maps obviously had a very special purpose. They were geographical maps of a fairly large region, with rivers, mountains, roads, and other landmarks drawn on them. Also, there were symbols and arrows identifying various locations and directions. These drawings were like those in a war room of a military headquarters where the commanding officers direct war operations.

Finally, this second vast army was commissioned to go forth with their written assignments until not one angel was left. Many of the large volumes had been emptied of their sealed documents, yet there were still more great books left. There was now only one army left in heaven.

...As the Lord began to assign the remaining forces of angels, this time He spoke more in detail as He handed each band their proper page. He was sending them to the churches, and they were to give wisdom and assistance to the people of God so that they could learn to do warfare in worship. They were told to teach them the music of heaven, and release a new anointing in the worship that would cause great fear to come into the ranks of the enemies of God....

Rolland continues:

Just as suddenly as this vision began, it ended as I found myself back in the car. For several minutes I could not move. Then, as the surroundings became familiar again, I tried to speak, but I could not control my mouth. The feeling in my lips and tongue was similar to having received a shot of Novocain.

It was obvious to everyone in the car that something very unusual had just occurred. They were all talking at once, trying to understand what had happened, but I could not speak for some time. Slowly the numbness in my mouth began to subside, but I was so deeply shaken by what I had seen I could not describe it to them.

Nothing even remotely like this had ever happened to me before in my entire life. I spoke a few sentences, but I was unsuccessful in explaining to them what I had seen.

Rolland rode in the car with his friends until they reached their destination, which was the city of Zagreb. He was so overwhelmed that he could hardly eat or sleep. He was convinced that the next day, they would hear on the news that World War III had begun.

But no war was declared, and he and Oke traveled on to Germany to teach at two conferences. The two of them spent every spare moment on their faces in their room, beseeching God to explain this angelic encounter.

The second conference was for Christian men and women from the United States armed forces, some with high-ranking positions. The sessions were held at an old mountain hotel, the Eagle's Nest, a place that had been built by Hitler for his most trusted officers. Rolland spoke to them about spiritual warfare and intercession, and he mentioned his recent experience, although he hesitated to "corrupt" such a holy experience by talking about it very much.

It was as they were all sharing Communion at the last session that, Rolland recounts, "the Lord Jesus opened my understanding and spoke softly into my heart."

> He began to explain what I had seen in the vision in detail. He spoke with a voice which expressed deep satisfaction and firmness. "What you saw," He said, "was not the angels going into battle alone. I was sending them to My servants all over the world. Today I have found faithful and trustworthy men and women all over the world.
>
> "Just as the military must subject soldiers to very severe tests to verify their trustworthiness with the secrets of war, defenses, weaponry, and battle plans, so I have also subjected my servants to the most severe tests for faithfulness. Now, I have, for the first time in the history of the world, such people positioned in every part of the entire globe."

My heart beat rapidly, and I rejoiced as the Lord opened my understanding. He said, "The angels were sent to My trusted servants. I have ordered My angels to reveal My deep secrets, My battle plans for the final war to overthrow the forces of all My enemies. The heavenly army will be on assignment to fight together with them. They will teach them wisdom much as I sent them to teach Daniel wisdom while he was in captivity. These trusted servants will not reveal My plans to the enemy! They will obey Me!"

Jesus continued to speak deep into my heart. "The maps you saw were the assignments to My servants. The angels were sent to deliver them. Every geographical area in the world is included. These are My officers, ready to assume the command of My army. These are captains, called to raise up the army of God in their territory and lead them into battle to take the region over which I have given them authority. There is much more, but I will tell you more when you need to know."

All during 1984 I waited for more from the Lord. Then, suddenly, on New Year's Eve of that year the Lord spoke again. Jesus said, "Those who were given these assignments will begin to develop strategies of prayer and evangelism for whole nations, multi-national regions, and whole continents. Networks will be formed among vast numbers of God's servants and will stretch out over the whole earth in mighty 'outreaches.' Even global strategies will be given."

All this was deeply moving down in my soul. I rejoiced. I hoped. I expected to see these things begin to happen at any moment.

Here we are, more than two decades down the road since that time. And yet, I think we can say with assurance that such regional and global strategies have been given to groups of people who have responded obediently. What Rolland Smith saw in a little yellow European car and at the Eagle's Nest was true. The fact that so much of the activity of the angelic army has been behind the scenes does not weaken the reality of what God is doing in these End Times.

We are the generation to whom these strategies are being given. We are the people, and this is the time. We are the church that is positioned to receive wisdom from God so that we can do our part in His plan.

I speak forth right now, as more pages are being handed out—"We *will* follow! We *will* obey!"

Yes, Jacob's ladder is still coming down today as heaven's angels keep on ascending and descending. Unending worship proceeds from this angelic choir to the One who sits upon the throne. And God's manifest presence, plans, and purposes keep on tumbling down into a time space world. Indeed, we are not alone. Help is on the way!

> *Come, Lord Jesus; come quickly, come! It's all about You. It's not about us, and it's not even about Your angels. It's Your kingdom that's coming, Lord. Fulfill Your promises. Execute Your End-Time plans! We stand before You, as ready as we can be. Prepare us; make us part of Your army; keep us alert and responsive to You. We love You! Highest praises to You. Amen!*

NOTES

Chapter 1 • Jacob's Ladder Keeps Coming Down

1. "Blessed Assurance" by Fanny J. Crosby (1820–1915). Public domain.

2. Matthew Henry, *Matthew Henry's Commentary on the Whole Bible: New Modern Edition,* Electronic Database (Peabody, MA: Hendrickson Publishers, Inc., 1991), excerpted from commentary on Genesis 28.

3. H. A. Baker, *Visions Beyond the Veil* (Tonbridge, England: Sovereign World, 2000), 40. Used with permission.

4. Ibid., 42–43.

5. Ibid., 55.

6. Retold from chapter 3 of my book *Kneeling on the Promises* (Grand Rapids, MI: Baker/Chosen Books, 1999), 65–66, and from my book *Exodus Cry* (Ventura, CA: Regal Books, 2001), 166–167.

7. Shawn Bolz, *Keys to Heaven's Economy: An Angelic Visitation from the Minister of Finance* (North Sutton, NH: Streams Publishing House, 2005), 17–18. Used with permission.

8. Ibid., 33.

9. Ibid., 34.

10. Ibid., 45.

11. Pascal P. Parente, *Beyond Space: A Book About Angels* (Rockford, IL: Tan Books and Publishers, 1973), 14–15.

Chapter 2 • My Personal Angelic Encounters

1. "Come, Thou Fount of Every Blessing" by Robert Robinson (1735–1860). Public domain.

Chapter 3 • Invaded!

1. "Spirit of God, Descend Upon My Heart" by George Croly (1780–1860). Public domain.

Chapter 4 • The Nature of These Celestial Beings

1. "Angels, From the Realms of Glory" by James Montgomery (1771–1854). Public domain.

2. Parente, *Beyond Space*, 18–19.

3. Martin Luther, *Table Talk*, trans. William Hazlitt (Gainesville, FL: Bridge-Logos, 2004), sec. 565.

4. John Calvin, *Institutes of the Christian Religion*, trans. Henry Beveridge (Grand Rapids, MI: Wm. B. Eerdmans Publishing Co., 1989), 1.14.5, 6, 9.

5. Margaret Barker, *An Extraordinary Gathering of Angels* (London: MQ Publications, 2004), 10.

6. Billy Graham, *Angels: God's Secret Agents* (Nashville, TN: Thomas Nelson/W Publishing Group, 1995), 30.

7. *Encyclopedia Mythica Online*, s.v. "Angels" (by Rabbi Geoffrey W. Dennis), http://www.pantheon.org/articles/a/angels.html (accessed September 29, 2006).

8. Danny Steyne, "Angels in Bennington, Vermont," GreatestAwakening.com, http://www.greatestawakening.com/angelsinbennington.htm (accessed October 9, 2006). Used with permission.

9. Ibid.

10. Ibid.

Chapter 5 • The Characteristics of Angels

1. "Ye Watchers and Ye Holy Ones," text by John Athelstan Laurie Riley (1858–1945). From *The English Hymnal*, copyright © Oxford University Press 1906. All rights reserved. Used by permission.

2. *Catholic Encyclopedia Online*, s.v. "Angels," http://www.newadvent.org/cathen/01476d.htm (accessed November 27, 2006).

3. Ibid. Also see, Thomas Aquinas, *Summa Theologica*, rev. ed., trans. Fathers of the English Dominican Province, 1.108, http://www.newadvent.org/summa/1108.htm (accessed March 8, 2007).

4. According to the *Catholic Encyclopedia Online*, "The only Scriptural names furnished of individual angels are Raphael, Michael, and Gabriel, names which signify their respective attributes. Apocryphal Jewish books, such as the Book of Enoch [and Esdras], supply those of Uriel and Jeremiel, while many are found in other apocryphal sources, like those Milton names in 'Paradise Lost.'"

5. Anna Rountree, *The Heavens Opened* (Lake Mary, FL: Charisma House, 1999).

6. You can read the Book of Enoch online by going to http://www.heaven.net .nz/writings/thebookofenoch.htm.

7. Roland Buck, *Angels on Assignment* (New Kensington, PA: Whitaker House, 1979), 165–167. Used with permission.

8. Coptic Orthodox Church Network, "The Coptic Church and Dogmas," 3.2, http://www.copticchurch.net/topics/thecopticchurch/church3-2.html (accessed November 30, 2006).

Chapter 6 • Angelic Assignments

1. "God, That Madest Earth and Heaven" by Reginald Heber (1783–1826). Public domain.

2. Terry Law, *The Truth About Angels* (Lake Mary, FL: Charisma House, 1994, 2006), 173–175.

3. "I've Got a Real, Live Angel" by Gloria Farah. Reprinted with permission from *Guideposts*. Copyright © 1993 by Guideposts Associates, Carmel, New York 10512. All rights reserved.

4. Ibid., 48.

5. Douglas Connelly, *Angels Around Us* (Downers Grove, IL: InterVarsity, 1994), 105–106.

6. Mary K. Baxter, with Dr. T. L. Lowery, *A Divine Revelation of Angels* (New Kensington, PA: Whitaker House, 2003), 186–187. Used with permission.

7. Paul Keith Davis, "As I Was With Moses," in WhiteDove Ministries November 2005 E-Newsletter, December 8, 2005, http://www .whitedoveministries.org/content/NewsItem.phtml?art=292&c=0&id= 30&style= (accessed December 8, 2006).

Chapter 7 • Jesus and the Ministering Angels

1. "I Stand Amazed in the Presence" by Charles H. Gabriel (1856–1932). Public domain.

2. "Angels We Have Heard on High," traditional French carol. Public domain.

3. "Angels, From the Realms of Glory" by James Montgomery (1771–1854). Public domain.

4. "While Shepherds Watched Their Flocks" by Nahum Tate (1652–1715). Public domain.

5. "Hark! The Herald Angels Sing" by Charles Wesley (1707–1788). Public domain.

Chapter 8 • Modern-Day Reports of Angelic Encounters

1. "It Came Upon a Midnight Clear" by Edmund H. Sears (1810–1876). Public domain.

2. Corrie ten Boom, *A Prisoner and Yet...* (Fort Washington, PA: Christian Literature Crusade, 1990), as quoted in Graham, *Angels: God's Secret Agents*, 139–141. Used with permission of CLC Publishers.

3. Graham, *Angels: God's Secret Agents*, 156–157.

4. As told in Buck, *Angels on Assignment*, 183–184.

5. Sandie Freed, "Co-Laboring With the Angels," on The Elijah List, July 8, 2006, http://www.theelijahlist.com/words/display_word/4259 (accessed July 9, 2006). Used with permission.

6. Bill Yount, "Something Sweeter Than Chocolate Is Now Coming Forth Out of Hershey, Pennsylvania...a Womb of 'Healing and Cures' for the Nations Is Now Opening," on The Elijah List, November 18, 2005, http://www.theelijahlist.com/words/display_word/3590 (accessed August 10, 2006). Used with permission.

7. Cindy Jacobs, *The Supernatural Life* (Ventura, CA: Regal Books, 2005), 130–131. Used with permission.

8. Law, *The Truth About Angels*, 42–43.

Chapter 9 • Discerning the Angelic Presence

1. "A Mighty Fortress Is Our God" by Martin Luther (1483–1586). Public domain.

Chapter 10 • Angelic Intervention Through Intercession

1. "Prayer Is the Soul's Sincere Desire" by James Montgomery (1771–1854). Public domain.

2. James W. Goll, *The Prophetic Intercessor* (Grand Rapids, MI: Chosen Books, 2007).

3. Shawn Bolz, "The Key of Breakthrough," on The Elijah List, July 3, 2006, http://www.elijahlist.com/words/display_word/4248 (accessed November 20, 2006). Used with permission.

Chapter 11 • The Work of Angels and the Nation of Israel

1. "All Glory, Laud, and Honor" by Theodulph of Orleans (c. 821). Public domain.

2. The twenty-four books of the Hebrew Bible (Tanakh) that became the Old Testament of our Christian Bible include: the five Books of Moses (the Pentateuch, or Torah)—Genesis, Exodus, Leviticus, Numbers, and Deuteronomy; eight Books of the Prophets—Joshua, Judges, Samuel (1 and 2 Samuel), Kings (1 and 2 Kings), Isaiah, Jeremiah, Ezekiel, and The Twelve (Trei-Assar) or the minor prophets; and eleven Books of the Writings—Psalms, Proverbs, Job, Song of Songs, Ruth, Lamentations, Ecclesiastes, Esther, Daniel, Ezra, Nehemiah, and Chronicles (1 and 2 Chronicles). The twelve books of the minor prophets include Hosea, Joel, Amos, Obadiah, Jonah, Micah, Nahum, Habakkuk, Zephaniah, Haggai, Zechariah, and Malachi. The Hebrew Books of Samuel, Kings, Ezra/Nehemiah, and Chronicles are each divided into two books in the Christian Bible.

3. This information comes from Appendix 2 of Gary Kinnaman, *Angels Dark and Light* (Ann Arbor, MI: Servant/Vine, 1994), 221.

4. Lance Lambert, *Battle for Israel* (Eastbourne, East Sussex, England: Kingsway Publications, 1975), 9, 11–13. Used with permission.

5. Ibid., 13–14.

6. Ibid., 17–18.

7. Ibid., 111.

8. Bill Yount, "The 'Esthers' Are Now Being Summoned to Come to Jerusalem to Stand Before the King...for Such a Time as This," on The Elijah List, August 18, 2006, http://www.elijahlist.com/words/display_word/4395 (accessed March 19, 2007). Used with permission.

Chapter 12 • Angels, the Harvest, and the End Times

1. "Rejoice, the Lord is King" by Charles Wesley (1707–1788). Public domain.

2. Ian Andrews, e-mail message to author, March 16, 2006. Used with permission.

3. Paul Keith Davis, "The Angel Stated That His Name Is 'Breakthrough!'" on The Elijah List, April 4, 2006, http://www.elijahlist.com/words/display_word/3959 (accessed March 19, 2007). Used with permission.

4. Rolland Smith, *Watchman Ministry Manual*. No further publishing information available. Reprinted with permission of Carrie J. Smith. All quotes from this account refer to this title.

Scripture Index

For More Information

Dr. James (Jim) W. and Michal Ann Goll are the cofounders of **Encounters Network**. They are members of the **Harvest International Ministries** Apostolic Team and contributing writers for *Kairos* **magazine** and other periodicals. Michal Ann is the founder of **Compassion Acts** reaching out to the poor of the earth. James is also an instructor in the **Wagner Leadership Institute,** member of the **Apostolic Council of Prophetic Elders,** and chairman of **TheCall** board. James and Michal Ann have four wonderful children and live in the beautiful rolling hills of Franklin, TN.

James has produced several study guides on subjects such as Equipping in the Prophetic, Blueprints for Prayer, and Empowered for Ministry—all available through the Encounters Resource Center.

Books by James W. and Michal Ann Goll

Fire on the Altar

The Lost Art of Intercession

Exodus Cry

Elijah's Revolution

The Coming Prophetic Revolution

*Women on the Frontlines—
a Call to Courage*

A Call to the Secret Place

Intercession

The Beginner's Guide to Hearing God

The Seer

God Encounters

Praying for Israel's Destiny

The Seer 40-Day Devotional Journal

The Lost Art of Practicing His Presence

Compassion

The Prophetic Intercessor

*Shifting Shadows of Spiritual
Experiences*

Angelic Encounters

For more information contact:
Encounters Network
P. O. Box 1653 • Franklin, TN 37075
Office Phone: 615-599-5552 • Office Fax: 615-599-5554
For orders call: 877-200-1604

For more information to sign up for their monthly e-mail communiques, visit their Web site at www.encountersnetwork.com or e-mail: info@encountersnetwork.com.

Additional Resources by
James W. & Michal Ann Goll

Prophetic Encounters

Featuring James W. Goll
Music by John Belt
Be prepared to receive a Prophetic Encounter as James W. Goll shares stories, and personal experiences, reads scripture and releases prayers of impartation. Titles include: Beautiful, Bread of His Presence, Rock the Nations, Over Here, Dread Champions, Giants of Faith, Days of Acceleration, The Golden Anointing, and many more...

$15.00

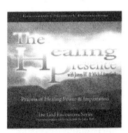

The Healing Presence

Featuring James W. & Michal Ann Goll
Music by John Belt
Receive God's Healing Presence as James W. & Michal Ann Goll read scripture, share stories, and release prayers of impartation. "The Lord really visited us in this recording!"
Titles include: The Hem of His Garment, The Day of Healing, How Lovely, The Healing River, and many more...

$15.00

Invitation to Intimacy

Featuring - James W. Goll & John Belt
Goll was caught up into another realm. Over 60 minutes of prophetic, spontaneous worship and teaching with keyboard and instrumentation in the background. Soak with this one!

$22.00

Prayers for Israel

Featuring - by James W. Goll
"Prayers For Israel" is one in a series of recordings focused specifically on praying biblical prayers for the nation and people of Israel. By using the biblical text as a track, James W. Goll prays from the Word as it is written, while still allowing for the freedom to launch out into Spirit-led spontaneity and personalized application. Following the practice of the ancients, each one of these prayers is set in the context of inspired musical accompaniment.

$12.00

For Additional Products by James W. and Michal Ann Goll

Visit www.jamesgoll.com | Call 1~877~200~1604

Study Guides by James W. Goll

Over the years, James W. Goll has taught these practical tools to help people all over the world learn a prophetic lifestyle. The comprehensive study guides in this series can be used either for individual study or with a class or small group. Following each detailed lesson are simple questions for reflection. As you work through these lessons, you will be inspired to take your place in God's prophetic army.

Equipping in the Prophetic | Enlisting a Prophetic Army

Prophetic Foundations

The first of this series on the prophetic. These 12 lessons include: For the Many - Not the Few, The History of the Prophetic, Intimacy in the Prophetic, Power & Perils of the Prophetic Spirit Seven Expressions of the Prophetic Spirit, Prophesy Life, The Prophetic Song of the Lord, and more...

$15.00

Experiencing Dreams & Visions

This is the second Guide in the series. These 12 lessons include: God's Multi-faceted Voice, Visionary Revelation, Journaling, Tools For Interpreting Revelation, Dream Language, Receiving and Judging Revelation, Wisdom in Handling Revelation, Dream Language I & II, Tips for Interpratations , and more...

$15.00

Prophetic Maturation

This is the third Guide in the series. These 12 lessons Include: Called Into Character, From Character to Commissioning, Seizing your Prophetic Destiny Parts 1 & 2, The Cross - The Prophetic Lifestyle, Four levels of Prophetic Ministry, The Seer and the Prophet: Similarities and Differences, and more...

$15.00

Understanding Supernatural Encounters

This is the fourth Guide in the series. These 12 lessons Include: Keys to the Supernatural, How to Receive Revelation, Demonstrating Three Models, The Deception of the Anointing, Levels Of Supernatural Visions Parts 1 & 2, Trances Defined, Ministry and Function of Angels, Current Day Accounts of Angelic Activity, and more...

$15.00